The Way
of Christ

Thou art the Way
Had'st Thou been nothing but the goal,
I cannot say
If Thou hadst ever met my soul.

Alice Meynell, 1847-1922

Daniel C. Whitaker

Rocky Comfort Press

Daniel C. Whitaker

copyright 2018

ISBN-13: 978-1727062694

Rocky Comfort Press

Dedicated to Joyce, my beloved wife of 55 years,

and the gifts of our lives together, John and Charles

Contents

Introduction

Words, words, words. Mine always fall short of the unsearchable riches of which I try to speak in all of my sermons. But I have tried. I've studied books, attended scores of preaching workshops, tried to do it like the masters. My failure is not for lack of earnest effort, but rather in the *size* of the thing. Before the great immensities of our faith "words strain, crack and sometimes break, under the burden" (T. S. Eliot). I invite you, then, to let the Spirit intercede for both of us, commending my creaky, straining words to you with sighs deeper than all our words.

anno Domini 2018

Emmanuel: God with Us

All this took place to fulfil what the Lord had spoken by the prophet: Behold, a virgin shall conceive and bear a son, and his name shall be called Emmanuel, which means God with us. Matthew 1:22-23

As I ponder this text two stories come to mind: Wallace Stevens, in a quirky poem, *"Anecdote of the Jar,"* writes

I placed a jar in Tennessee,
And round it was upon a hill.
It made the slovenly wilderness
Surround that hill.
The wilderness rose up to it,
And sprawled around, no longer wild . . .

The other story is more straight-forward. A father took his little girl to the seashore. It was her first time, and scared as she was, she refused the slightest venture toward the water. But then her father took a toy tea kettle they'd brought, filled it from the ocean, and together they played with it. They poured the water over their feet and even made a moat to circle her little sand castle. Almost magically the girl's fear was forgotten and she was soon frolicking in the waves.

You see the point of those two stories. Both wilderness and ocean were altered by a human touch. Wild, once-dangerous worlds were tamed, and seen with new eyes. In a far deeper sense, Jesus' incarnate entry into human life has transformed our very planet. His personal, human bond with a land and a people fits him for that lofty title which our faith assigns him: Emmanuel, God with us. Through Jesus the high, transcendent God stooped low to share our human journey, to identify with us. The supreme treasure of Advent is that those earth-visiting feet actually walked with us. Exposed and vulnerable in all of our wilderness places, we longed for a presence, a voice, a face. The bruised, beleaguered Job speaks for all of us when life has bottomed out: *"O that I knew where I might find him!"* Him! Him, so Sphinx-like in his sometimes-silence.

Years ago I was at a Baptist Student Union banquet at the University of Florida, slated to speak. During the meal an anxious knot of students came to where I was eating and asked if I would talk to a crazy drifter who had come off the streets to the student center. When I met the man-- apparently high, deeply agitated-- he kept yelling out his aching question: "Where is He?! Where is He?!" It was like an echo of old Thomas Wolfe's abandoned cry: "Lost! O lost!"

That cosmic ache was fully addressed when God poured his own vital being into the particular person of Jesus of Nazareth. It was a pivotal turning point. Earlier, the Unseen Mystery had tried over and again to reach us:

In many and varied ways God spoke of old to our fathers by the prophets; but in these last days he has spoken to us by a Son . . .

Can't you hear the rumble of great tectonic plates as they shift toward a huge and greater redemption? This Emmanuel Jesus made God unforgettably present: a face seen, a voice heard, a touch felt. His birthplace was a real and palpable cattle stall, where you almost smell the hay and see the croker sacks piled against the wall. His later workplace was formed along any dusty roadway, or maybe down the gravelly venue of that never-distant seashore. All this rightly so. For if you can ever get truth focused in an actual person and place, it becomes dramatically accessible. Emmanuel gives to God at long last a face: *No one has ever seen God; the only Son, who is in the bosom of the Father, he has made him known (John 1:8)*

So there you have it: the wild surmise of Christian faith, our brash and daring claim, that in Jesus, God himself is with us. It has been challenged down the centuries. From Celsus to Bertrand Russell, great fiery torches of denial have flamed out against it. More often, myriads of little-faiths—of which we ourselves are sometimes a reluctant part—smother the claim by the slow, smokeless burning of disbelief. So against the fervent assaults of formal atheism, or the subtler dismissals of our practical atheism, how does Christian faith affirm that Jesus is Emmanuel? Where Emmanuel? How Emmanuel?

He is with us in our sin. Jesus launched his public ministry with his baptism by John at the Jordan. Matthew tells us of the Baptist's strong misgivings: "I need to be baptized by you. Do you come to me?" But at Jesus' firm insistence John baptized him in the waters of repentance, standing amid the dripping penitents. That act was a profound symbol of solidarity with sinners. He bonded himself with the lost and wayward, standing where they stood. It became his signature role: friend of sinners. That title began, of course, as a sneering put-down, but forgiven sinners made it into their heartfelt compliment.

He stood once with an adulteress. Caught in her shame, she was hustled before him by scribes and Pharisees: "Moses commanded stoning; what do you say?" After a measured pause and a long, reflective silence came his verdict: "Let him who is without sin cast the first stone." As the crowd melted away, this guilty woman becomes a proxy for all sinners, hearing the grace of the everlasting mercy: "Neither do I condemn you. Go and sin no more."

What is the worst thing you ever did? What do you regret, wish to call back, long to undo? What hateful word, what ugly betrayal, what wounding act? The Emmanuel Christ stands beside you in the profound empathy of repentance. Hebrews portrays him as a great high priest who shared our human nature, and knows our weakness, temptation and guilt. Yet he is not ashamed to call us sisters and brothers.

My mother once phoned to tell of my younger brother's arrest and jailing on serious drug charges. I remember well my sense of shame when I saw him at the local jail. Who sees me? Do they know me? Do they think I am some low-lifer too? But our Emmanuel stands with sinners unashamed! From his baptism until his death between two thieves, he was numbered with the transgressors.

But there is more. **Emmanuel is beside us in our ordinary joys and our workaday pursuits.** Brother Lawrence helped me see it. At Stetson University I was a student worker at the library. My supervisor, an unmarried woman of late middle age, was not easy to work for. She was stern, sour and lacking all the pleasant graces, and made me wonder if she was sour because she never married, or never married because she was sour. However, upon my graduation she gave me, all unexpected, two books as a gift. One was a classic devotional work, **The Practice of the Presence of God,** written by a 17th century monk called Brother Lawrence. He seems to have worshiped more in the kitchen where he worked, than in the cathedral. He could pray with another,

> *Lord of all pots and pans and things,*
> *Make me a saint by getting meals*
> *And washing up the plates!*

Here are his own words:

> The time of business does not with me differ from the
> time of prayer; and in the noise and clatter of my kitch-
> en, while several persons are at the same time calling
> for different things, I possess God in as great a tranquil-
> ity as if I were upon my knees at the blessed sacrament.

To know the presence of Emmanuel in the daily round hallows and dignifies everything. We can affirm with Isaac Watts, about every step of our human journey, "We're marching through Emmanuel's ground." That joyous presence among us sanctifies human potential and destiny. Thomas Traherne put it tellingly:

> I had never known the dignity of my nature hadst thou
> not esteemed it; I had never seen or understood its glory
> hadst thou not assumed it.

Jesus' embrace of our humanity, his incarnate presence within it, opens our eyes to an underestimated glory. I once read that a Cornishman, who had been chided by a rude visitor for the drabness and insignificance of his country,answered quietly, "My lord, something over a hundred years ago a man named John Wesley came to these parts." Let that rustic parable lead us into the higher magnitude of Alice Meynell's tribute to the incarnate Christ: *Our wayside planet...bears, as chief treasure, one forsaken grave.* In Jesus---Emmanuel---we see and measure God's estimation of his creation, his unwavering bond of love for the world he made.

But there is more. **Emmanuel stands beside us in trial**

and adversity. When Saul was harrowing the infant church, hounding believers to prison and even death, he set out for Damascus with his grim subpoenas. But on the way it was Saul himself who was arraigned, and by a probing question: "Why do you persecute me?" said the heavenly voice. "Why persecute *me*?" Saul learned in that encounter that to touch one of Christ's own was to touch him. So identified was he with his followers that to attack them was tantamount to attacking him. Few of us will ever face persecution, but those who have known him in the fellowship of his suffering did discover the Presence. Samuel Rutherford, imprisoned in Aberdeen for his faith, bore witness in a letter to a fellow church member: "Jesus Christ came to my cell last night and every stone glowed like a ruby."

The more typical trials we face are the more ordinary, *"the heart-ache and the thousand natural shocks that flesh is heir to."* The birth of a Down Syndrome child; a parent with dementia; a lost job. Emmanuel's own are not immune to the still, sad music of humanity, but he remains their steadfast companion in the fellowship of agony. Your son needs drug rehab; your daughter is anorexic; you marriage crashes and burns. But he is there. Always Emmanuel.

And still there is more. **He is with us in grief and loss.** He understands the tears of things. "A man of sorrows and acquainted with grief." Once he watched a youth he loved, in search of eternal life, give up sadly and walk away. He wept at the graveside of Lazarus, his friend. And at the end he wept again for a city, so blind to its peril. No tragic loss could escape his notice, no need slip by his care.

Dr. William Hull, my graduate supervisor of yesteryear, is now dying with Lou Gehrig's Disease. He announced the news publicly at its outset. Ever the teacher, he wanted his struggle to be a forthright seminar where he would report candidly his existential battles with issues of mortality and faith. On the third anniversary of his diagnosis, he gave a public update: Hospice had been called in; he could never again stand or walk; his arms had become broomsticks; an eating tube was in place, andan oxygen tube; his ability to communicate was under severe threat: he can barely talk write or type, and they too will soon be gone.

Spiritually, as he hears "time's winged chariot hurrying near," Dr. Hull's thoughts turn to death's ultimate meaning. He immerses himself in the great literature, music and poetry that abound on that universal subject. In a revealing glimpse, he shares his reliance on the Emmanuel presence. As his brief chapter draws to a close, he sings to himself that sturdy Welsh hymn:

> *When I tread the verge of Jordan,*
> *Bid my anxious fears subside;*
> *Bear me through the swelling current,*
> *Land me safe on Canaan's side.*

By now you see my premise clearly: every human step we take is taken on Emmanuel's ground. He is with us in sin and failure; in our workaday pursuits; in our sorest trials; and in our deep griefs We feel a bond with him in our aching aloneness. Has not God , of high, hidden mystery, stooped low in Emmanuel to let us put our hands on his face? I concede that it sounds like a placebo, a comforting illusion, or maybe like Linus' blanket. Aware of the enticements of such fantasies, still I choose to believe that Emmanuel is really there. I have set all my hopes on him. No proof, of course. Only trust. He came to our wilderness. Not a jar, but a Son, whose very last words are Emmanuel to the bone: I am with you always! Always!

All's Lost

I have received only one telegram in my life. It came at a moment of joy, and the small yellow note seemed to intensify the joy. What with email, chat rooms, texting and twittering, telegrams must be going the way of kerosene lamps. But then, because every word was expensive, telegrams enforced a wonderful economy of words. I remember reading that when Horatio Spafford's wife and four daughters were caught in an Atlantic storm while sailing to England, only Mrs. Spafford survived. When she reached Dublin and wired the wrenching news back to her husband in Chicago, her grief was compressed into just two dreadful words: "Saved alone."

I am called to put the gospel into words. Sometimes, in a world glutted with books and words, with radio words and television words, with website words and talk show words, I despair of words. How, I ask myself, could the gospel be pared back to a single telegram? How could the good news be distilled into a kind of Western Union word from God? I don't know how you would do it, but here is my attempt: *All's lost; all's found*

What follows are two sermons, each one being half of my distilled gospel.

All's Lost

> *For as by a man came death, by a man has come also the resurrection of the dead. For as in Adam all die, so also in Christ shall all be made alive. (I Corinthians 15: 21-22)*

The coming of Jesus Christ is supremely good news. But the only way to comprehend the extent and power of that good news is to know the hideous strength of the bad news. Paul traces the collective anguish of our human story back to a point very soon after Eden's first morning. The primal couple, Adam and Eve, disobey their Creator, fall under his curse, and are expelled from their lush paradise. In old Vance Havner's folksy summary, our first parents ate us out of house and home.

The Genesis story is full of primal symbolism as it accounts for the root of man's universal brokenness and alienation. It never poses as empirical historical research, like some modern epidemiologist seeking to track down the actual spinach farm that triggered a national outbreak of E-coli. It is, rather, a theological, mytho-poeic effort to tell the truth about us all at a level far deeper than mere history. The prohibited fruit was from a stock no nursery grows. The species: Tree of the Knowledge of Good and Evil. The serpent , defying all known herpetology on earth, talks to Eve with the charm and wit of a Casanova. The very name Adam means man or mankind in Hebrew usage.

The story describes what Christian theology will later call the Fall. Although "Fall" is not a biblical term, it is an apt description of Paul's use of the Genesis story. He sees Adam as the head of a fallen humanity. Though he never spells out the precise mechanism, Adam's sin ensnares us all in guilt, alienation and death. Paul sees all mankind caught in a mysterious, dark undertow that sucks us, even against our will, into our own individual renditions of Adam's trespass.

Carlyle Marney was once asked, "Where is the Garden of Eden?"

"Two-fifteen Elm Street, Knoxville, Tennessee," he said.

"But I thought it was somewhere in Asia," said the enquirer.

"Well," he answered, "you couldn't prove it by me, because it was there on Elm Street, when I was a boy that I stole a quarter from my mama's purse and went down to the store and bought me some candy. I ate it, but then was so ashamed that I went back and hid in the closet. It was there that Mama said, 'Where are you? Why are you hiding? What have you done?'"

The undertow, in Paul's view, spares no one. But this dark reality is not meant to nurture pessimism. It rather is a foil to make brighter the exultant optimism of his joyous gospel. To taste and see the benefits of the Second Adam, one must first own up to the fearful sway of the First Adam. So I turn now to our own darkness.

Nothing is better documented than evil in our world. If you see sin as an outworn Christian superstition, go spend time in a Holocaust museum. Or call back to memory these words, slowly: My Lai; Charles Manson; Timothy McVeigh: World Trade Center; Bernie Madoff. Sin is not an obsolete biblical theory. The monotonous, ages-old story of human folly, war and crime bears grim witness to its vigorous presence. The great writers chronicle it well enough: Shakespeare, Dostoevsky, Faulkner. Even its old Christian name is pressed into service: **The Fall** (Camus), **After the Fall** (Miller), and where we live now, **East of Eden** (Steinbeck).

The Enlightenment produced in the West, besides its glorious scientific achievements, an over-optimism about man's natural goodness. William Golding writes of his own outlook:

If you had met me before World War II, you would have found me to have been an idealist with a simple and naïve belief which many of my generation shared, especially in Europe. This naïve belief was that man was perfectible. We thought all you had to do was to remove certain inequities and provide practical sociological solutions, and man would have a perfect paradise on earth. From World War II we learned something. The war was unlike any other fought in Europe. It taught us not fighting, politics or the follies of nationalism, but about the given nature of man.

When Golding wrote his first novel, he described it as an attempt to trace the defects of society back to the defects of human nature. The novel tells of a large group of boys taken to an island paradise for their safety during war. These sunny, innocent youths, well educated and from solid families, quickly lose the veneer of civilization, to form rival war parties. They slide into bloodlust, mutilation and murder with a hurtling swiftness. In this new,luxuriant Eden, once again all's lost,and we seem to hear Paul's echoed stage whisper, "All have sinned and fall short of the glory of God."

Which sin, exactly, forms the fatal flaw in our nature? Pride is frequently named, and so is rebellion. I am drawn to the powerful case Graham Greene seems to make for *destruction*, the reversal of creation. I refer to his short story, **The Destructors**. Here he tells of a gang of boys in London, after World War II. They decide to destroy completely the house of an old man who lives in their neighborhood. They call him Old Misery. He is a retired decorator, of limited means, who took an old house damaged by bombs during the Blitz, and repaired it as well as he could afford. The house was built by Christopher Wren, and featured a spiral staircase. The neighbors knew nothing of this, but the old man had shown the inside of the house to one of the boys. The boy—called T by the gang—also was told by the old recluse that he was going away on a two-day holiday.

When he left for his trip, the gang broke into his house, bringing hammers, chisels, saws screwdrivers---anything they could find--- and the destruction began. They systematically defaced and demolished everything. Organized and eager, they pulled up flooring, kicked in door panels, sawed down the staircase, smashed the bath fixtures, and the kitchen china. "They worked with the seriousness of creators," wrote Greene. The sheer joy of destruction seemed to sustain their dark and twisted energy. They found Old Misery's life savings in a mattress. It amounted to 70 pounds. Hiding from the rest, he burned the notes one at a time. No theft in the ordinary sense: just ice-cold, unblinking destruction. The final devastation came when the gang tied carefully hidden ropes from the walls to a large lorry parked in the lot beside the house. When the unsuspecting driver started off in the lorry he heard the sound of a massive collapse as dust and debris filled the air. The young destructors' triumph was now complete.

Is *destruction* the cardinal sin, a demonic human urge to ravage and undo creation, to drag it back to formless chaos? None of us can say, of course.

John Claypool chooses *mistrust* at a primal level as the basic sin,. The serpent's spiel is that God's real reason for putting a certain fruit off limits was to guard his own status. He knows, the tempter assures Eve, that if they eat of the forbidden tree they will be like God himself. God's stated reasons can't be trusted; God only intends to eliminate possible rivals to his power and place.

Claypool illustrated the power of mistrust in his Beecher lectures. In a Midwest town two identical twin sons inherited their father's store. The two were unusually close, and were regarded in the town as models of close, warm relations as business partners. One morning a customer made a small purchase. The brother who waited on him wanted to chat as the customer left, so he just laid the dollar bill on top of the register and walked him to the door. Later he went to put the bill in the register, but it was not there. He asked his brother if he had put it in the register and he replied that he knew nothing of the missing bill. "That's funny. I distinctly remember putting the bill on the cash register, and no one has been here since," he said. If the minor mystery had been dropped right then, nothing would have come of it. But an hour later, with a hint of suspicion in his voice, the brother asked again, "Are you sure you didn't put that dollar in the register?" Catching the accusatory tone, his brother flared back in defensive anger.

This was the start of a growing rift. Their bond of trust was for the first time broken. Now, whenever the sore subject was broached again, new charges and countercharges bristled. Finally things got so bad that they dissolved the partnership. They ran a partition down the middle of their father's store, and set up rival shops. The old bond of harmony was replaced with fierce competition. Their vendetta even crept into the larger community, some siding with one twin, some with the other. This bitter division went on for twenty years.

Then one day a car from out of state pulled up to the stores. A well-dressed man went into one of the stores and asked the merchant how long he had been in business there. When he found out that it had been more than twenty years, the stranger said he wanted to settle an old score.

"About twenty years ago I was a drifter, broke and hungry. I hadn't eaten in three days. Walking down the back alley, I saw through the door a dollar bill on top of the register. Everybody in the store was up front. I had been raised a Christian, never stolen anything, but hunger won out and I took the dollar. That theft has bothered my conscience ever since, and I finally decided I would never be at peace until I faced up and made amends. I want to repay the dollar and whatever damages I've caused."

At that point the stranger saw the merchant shaking his head in dismay and beginning to weep. He took the stranger by the arm and said, "Would you go next door and repeat that same story? " He agreed to this, and saw, when he finished his tale, two men who looked remarkably alike, weeping side by side.

What if mistrust, then, is the central clue to our Fall. The serpent gave clear warning that God is not to be trusted. So then, if we are entirely on our own, must desperately fend for ourselves, must root-hog for our own well-being, then a cosmic suspicion of God's care is born. That toxin spreads, and soon mistrust, with its deadly ruin, invades the hills and hollows of the whole creation.

But suppose our ruin springs from yet another root. Reinhold Niebuhr comes near to persuading me that the trigger-point of sin resides in man's unique status within Creation. He is both finite creature, *and* made in God's image. Living in that burdensome balance produces inevitable anxiety. The constant temptation in that inherent anxiety is to deny one side or the other of the balance. To conclude that one is completely and only a creature leads to sin-via-sensualism, with its surrender to the beckonings of flesh. To conclude that one transcends creaturely status leads to sin-via-pride, with all of its lofty pretensions. Both options prove to be both pathetic and deadly.

We have looked at thoughtful efforts to solve the puzzle of sin's hideous strength. Still, I find no final solution. Though the Bible knows the potent reality of sin, its root is never given a name. The gospel is less intent on providing the schematics of sin's assault on the First Adam than in announcing the joy-ous rescue of the Second Adam. So in that same faith we dare to believe that our only health lies in facing honestly our sin. In the searching light of the altar we mourn our pitiful track record. The good we long so earnestly to do goes undone; the evil that we abhor, still we yield to. All's lost, all's lost.. But Oh, do brace yourselves for the coming glory: in Jesus Christ all's found!

All's Found

For as by a man came death, by a man has come also the res-
urrection of the dead. For as in Adam all die, so also in Christ
shall all be made alive.   (I Corinthians 15: 21-22)

The leaves of the New Testament rustle with the news:
All's found! All's found through Jesus Christ. In Paul's view,
Christ, by his death and resurrection, has become a dazzling
new Adam. Just as we all have been caught in a tangled solidarity with Adam's sin, so we find release and redemption through a
mystic unity with the Second Adam. In Paul's astonishing vision
a whole new creation has begun. Those "in Christ"have become
new creations. The old has passed away; the new has come. Already the entire cosmos groans in the birth pangs of a new creation, freed from its deadly bondage to decay.

Paul's images pour down like Niagara as he tells in his
letters our enviable status: *adopted into God's family; acquitted*
in heaven's tribunal; reconciled across walls of hatred and divi-
sion. Paradise lost becomes, through Him, Paradise regained.

No more let sins and sorrows grow,
Nor thorns infest the ground.
He comes to make his blessings flow
Far as the curse is found.

Paul's voice is not alone. The good news is an air for many voices. Hear Peter's ringing plaudits for this new people:

But you are a chosen race,
A royal priesthood,
A holy nation,
God's own people. (I Peter 2:9)

Or see wide-eyed John exclaiming,

See what love the Father has given us, that we should be called children of God. (I John 3:1)

Even the low-key, unflappable James designates them a New Israel as he calls Christians the Twelve Tribes of the Dispersion, destined, once they pass the test of trials, to receive God's promised crown of life.

John on Patmos exults in the benefits drawn from Him who loves us and has freed us from our sins by his blood and made us a kingdom, priests to his God and Father. (Revelation 1:5)

This chorus of witnesses unites in a single, wild surmise: a new humanity has been born. But we must be honest. A huge and urgent question hangs over our Christian manifesto. If we are indeed a new humanity, why do we fall so pitifully short of our high destiny? Why does the seed of the Second Adam seem so rag-tag and bobtail? Why does their track record over the centuries require so many apologies?

Findley Edge, a seminary prophet-teacher, wrestled with this question in his book, **The Greening of the Church**. He tells how as a student pastor in a small church he found most of his flock to be distressingly nominal and apathetic, luke-warm toward any sense of mission. They reflected far more of their culture's values than any vision of a new humanity. Edge's question becomes my own question: why do we follow so fitfully and sketchily our beloved progenitor?

Doug Watterson, a Baptist minister, relates his own de-flating encounter. Late one Saturday night as he drove home from the last service of a revival in North Florida, he saw a sailor hitchhiking on the road ahead of him. Being an old Navy man himself, he was an easy touch. He pulled over and picked him up. The sailor began immediately to brag about his Saturday night conquests, the booze, the women. To spare him later embarrassment from having told too much, Watterson introduced himself, adding pointedly that he was the pastor of First Baptist Church, Tallahassee. "Put 'er there," the sailor burst out, extending his hand heartily, "I'm a Baptist myself!"

The sad truth of this story is about me too, of course. We keep under-imagining our high calling; we keep under-living our true selves. Think only of the depressing monotony of scandals in the Protestant ministry, or of the high wall of official cover-up in Roman Catholic priestly predation. Both call back memories of Ezekiel's prophetic response to Israel's betrayal of Yahweh's holiness. "Stop profaning the holiness of God to outsiders by your sins! Live as if you are his people." Nietzsche's stinging gibe still touches a sensitive nerve: "Show me you are redeemed and I will believe in your redeemer."

Oh, yes, I know there are Christian men and women of fire, those rare and radiant new creations in Christ. I celebrate their love and saintliness. It is their scarcity that troubles me. Is there an honest way to explain the dismaying gap between the Bible's resounding claims of a new humanity and the ethical and spiritual failures of actual Christians?

The best word I have found on this dilemma came from the gifted expositor, C.F.D.Moule. He concluded that the strange thing about this new life claimed by Christians is that they have it, and have it not. They have to keep striving to become what, as they claim, they already are. He admits this paradox is is illogical and loaded with tension. It rests in the unceasing countercurrents of (1)the assurances of a whole new nature, and (2) the insistent ethical urging to try harder. In his Colossian letter Paul can say, *"You have died to the old self and its ways,"* then in the next breath say, *"Put to death all that is earthly in you."*

Clearly, we are dealing with a paradox. Becoming what we are is the painful, laborious work of a lifetime. But by another paradox, we find, even as we struggle,a strange peace, an assurance that the grace already given us is our hope and our confidence. All's found, yes. But not in a wrapped, and ribboned package: rather in a pathway and a process.

The new life in Christ begins in faith. We embrace God's call to return to Eden's first morning, all bright with obedience and trust. Having sighed so long for Eden, we can now go back to Paradise as children of a Second Adam. Ramakrishna's fable helps me get the feel of it.

A motherless tiger cub was adopted by goats. The cub learned everything from his new family: language, lifestyle, cuisine. He became, in his own mind, a goat. One day a king tiger appeared, and all the goats scattered in fear. The young tiger was afraid too, but also strangely unafraid. "What do you mean by this unseemly masquerade?", asked the king tiger. The cub's only response was to bleat nervously and nibble at the grass.

Then the great beast led him to a pool of water and made him look at the pair of them side by side, to draw his own conclusions. Still no recognition from the cub. The king tiger then gave him some raw meat to eat. At first he recoiled from the strange taste, but slowly awakening to the truth, he felt his blood warming. At last, lashing his tail and digging his claws into the earth, he raised his head high and the jungle trembled with his roar.

Our salvation is both the acceptance of a gracious gift, and a roar of discovery, an awakening to our truest identity. The faith that enables it, the sight that opens the way, however, is notoriously subject to weakness, and fainting fits. Herein lies the answer to why sin and error are so sadly evident in Christendom's annals, and more to the point, in our own lives. A maddening amnesia dogs our pathway. A hateful entropy can exhaust our spiritual fervor and deplete our finest intentions.

Prone to wander, Lord I feel it,
Prone to leave the God I love.

Everything runs down, it seems, even in this Land of the New Humanity. Robert Frost has given me an unforgettable phrase for this phenomenon:

Nature's first green is gold,
Her hardest hue to hold.
Her early leaf's a flower;
But only so an hour.
Then leaf subsides to leaf.
So Eden sank to grief,
So dawn goes down to day.
Nothing gold can stay.

The deep covenant pledge between Yahweh and Israel, for example, was gold that could not stay. So too, the golden exuberance of the Protestant reformation ran down and lost itself in the tedium of Scholastic pedantry. Again, the fervor of the intrepid Mayflower pilgrims quickly cooled in the next generation and soon slid into a Half-Way Covenant. Nothing gold can stay. Even Paul, who framed the soaring theology of the Second Adam, who boasted of its transforming power, also gave voice to its severe limits in his own experience:

> *I can will what is right, but I cannot do it. For I do not do the good I want, but the evil I do not want is what I do. (Romans 7)*

Our true hope for continued vitality in the new life in Christ lies in constant renewal. The prophets in every generation must keep leading us in a searching self-criticism. Informed and aware of past Christian compromise/ collusion with such evils as slavery, or colonialism, or militarism, or Caesaropapism and its later guises, we will pursue Christ's light on critical emerging issues. Shepherds of the new humanity will gently and courageously lead to better wisdom, light and love. Renewal! Renewal! For we have died to Adam's darkness in whatever current guise it may appear. We have been raised with Christ to bear the image of the Second Adam. And even if the gold of that new creation can never stay in its pristine splendor, it can be found anew. Over and over we can stir up the gift of God; again and again we can lift our drooping hands and strengthen our weak knees. On this very pathway we will travel until at last we reach that city. All's found! All's found!

Gratitude Is a Choice

Philippians 1: 12-18

I want to make a clearing in my heart and yours where genuine gratitude can grow. I am aware that all of us at times are fighting hard battles. But gratitude can be felt amid trouble if we learn the secret. The secret is that gratitude is always a choice.

The Apostle Paul shows us the way in his letter to the Philippians. Through the entire letter joy and thanksgiving toll like a bell. This comes as a surprise when one recalls Paul's first visit to plant a church there. Philippi had been no Camelot. There the city magistrates had Paul and Silas stripped and severely beaten with rods. They were then imprisoned.

Now, as he writes this joyous letter, he writes from prison. Even there he finds reasons to be glad. His imprisonment has actually advanced the gospel: the whole imperial guard, as well as others have learned that his imprisonment is for Christ; fellow believers, emboldened by his jailing, have dared to speak out courageously; and even though some proclaim Christ from envy and rivalry, others do it from love and goodwill; and even if Christ is preached from wrong motives, Paul will rejoice that

Christ is proclaimed. How can you conquer a spirit like that? Amid every hardship and difficulty his letter stands as a daunt-less ode to joy! It pulses with warm thanksgiving and joyous faith.

How can this be? The only answer I know is that grati-tude is a choice. It is a chosen response to the ups and downs that every person meets in life. Viktor Frankl was a survivor of the Nazi work camp at Auschwitz. In a book he wrote about that holocaust experience, he describes what he calls the last of the human freedoms. The Nazis took away nearly everything from these prisoners. They took their livelihood, their homes, their money, art, jewelry, and their personal plans. But there was one thing they could not take: the ability to choose one's attitude in those dehumanizing circumstances. Frankl observed a few in-mates, who, when work was done, would walk through those wretched huts comforting others. He saw others who, despite their own desperate hunger,gave someone weaker their last crust of bread.

I have come to believe that we all have this final freedom. We can choose our responses and attitudes towards whatever is our lot. Gratitude was the choice Paul made. It would have been easy to choose resentment or bitterness. Charles Dickens had a marvelous gift for character description. We all have habitual patterns of response to life. In his novel **David Copperfield** he portrayed old Mrs. Gummidge, a professional widow. She of-ten voiced her habitual complaint, "I'm a lone, lorn creetur," whimpering into her black silk hanky. It was her chronic search for sympathy and attention. She had experieced loss, and her response was to wallow in her pain.

Churchill told the story of the sailor who jumped into a dock to save a small boy from drowning. About a week later this sailor was accosted by the boy's mother. "Are you the man who picked my son out of the dock?" The sailor replied modestly, "That is true, ma'am." "Then you're the man I'm looking for. Where is his cap?" My guess is that ingratitude was her customary response to life. Her neurotic outlook is a spur to me to work harder on my own tattered track record. None of us get to write our own script about what life will bring, but we do get to choose our response.

I have felt the lift and light of those who learned the art of gratitude. The Separatist pilgrims of the Plymouth colony came in 1620 with 102 in their company. Only 50 survived the winter. But the following fall their gifted governor, William Bradford, proclaimed a day of thanksgiving. Having crossed "a vast & furious ocean," with its "periles & miseries," they had survived "a hidious & desolate wildernes, full of wild beasts and willd men." His chosen response was not a day of mourning for their losses, but a day of thanksgiving for God's providence. Sixteen years later, across the Atlantic in Eilenburg, Germany, Pastor Martin Rinkart buried some 4,500 victims of the plague in 1637. The Thirty Years' War, 1618-1648, was in full swing, with all its cruelties and suffering. It was about this time that he wrote his hymn, *"Now Thank We All Our God."* Given the scale of suffering and death all about him, the words of his hymn stand as a tribute to a sense of gratitude that nothing can conquer:

> *Now thank we all our God, with heart and hands and voices;*
> *Who wondrous things hath wrought, in whom the world rejoices;*
> *Who from our mother's arms, hath led us on our way*
> *With countless gifts of love, and still is ours today.*

Rinkart chose to focus on the feast about him, not the famine. A friend who grew up working in is father's cotton gin told me about Albert Lewis, a share cropper from the Keith community. In the late 1940's-early1950's some farmers still brought their cotton to the gin by mule and wagon, though most had trucks by then. Albert brought his in an older wagon with steel-rimmed wheels. Unlike the other wagons, his did not even have rubber tires. Besides getting his cotton ginned, Albert, who could not read or write, had my friend help him fill out his crop support program form for the government. My friend would read the questions : How many rooms does your house have? "Four." Do you have an indoor bathroom? "No, Sir." Do you have a refrigerator ? "No Sir." Running water? "No, Sir. I don't have any of them things, Jim." Then he said, "I got four daughters, and they're doing good in school. God shore been good to me, Jim."

Oh, yes. Gratitude is a choice. Sunday afternoons six or eight of us would lead a devotional service at Bolingreen Nursing Home, near our town of Forsyth. Once an older black man who lived there asked to sing for us. He stood there before us and sang from memory:

I *wanna thank You, thank You, thank You, for my journey;*
You brought me from a long, long way;
You brought me through the hills and the valleys
You brought me from a long, long way.
You brought me through sickness and sorrow;
You brought me from a long, long way.
I wanna thank You, thank You, thank You for my journey;
You brought me from a long, long way.

On and on he sang for a good while. Verse after verse with the same theme: God's helping providence through every trial and storm. This old gentleman had found the secret of gratitude. Even in the face of difficulties and hard knocks he was able to let songs of joy break forth. Gratitude is a choice, and it is found in unlikely places.

In his unique spiritual memoir, Frederick Buechner tells of
growing up in a home with no connection to formal religion.
Worship, prayer or religious training was not a part of his childhood or family experience. But some deep inner compass pointed him to gratitude as a fitting response to life. In the last years
of World War II he was in an infantry battalion training near An-
niston, Alabama. It was winter as he was on bivouac, with a cold
rain drizzling, and everything was mud. The sun had gone down
as they sat in army fatigues, eating supper from their mess kits.
He had finished his, but was still hungry. He noticed a man near-
by had finished, and had a raw turnip that he was not going to
eat. When he asked if he could have it , the man tossed it over to
him. He missed the catch and it fell to the ground. But he wanted
it so badly that he picked it up and started eating it anyway, mud
and all. Let Buechner finish the story in his own words:

> And then, as I ate it, time deepened and slowed
> down again. With a lurch of the heart that is real to me
> still, I saw suddenly, almost as if from beyond time al-
> together, that not only was the turnip good, but the mud
> was good too, even the drizzle and cold were good, even
> the army that I had dreaded for months. Sitting there in
> the Alabama winter with my mouth full of cold turnip
> and mud, I could see at least for a moment how if you
> ever took truly to heart the ultimate goodness and joy of
> things, even at their bleakest, the need to praise someone
> or something for it would be so great that you might even
> have to go out and speak of it to the birds of the air.

No wonder the Psalms are filled with the call to praise:
*"O taste and see that the Lord is good." "Bless the Lord, O my
soul, and all that is within me, bless his holy name."* As a young
new Christian C.S. Lewis was bothered by the Psalms' ceaseless
call to praise the Lord. It suggested to him a God akin to a dicta-

tor, or a cheap politician who needed to be surrounded by servile toadies to flatter him constantly. Soon Lewis came to see that we must praise, not because God needs it, but because we need it. There is an inborn need for us all to admire and recognize true excellence. A stunning painting, an exquisite piece of music, a superb book call out to be appreciated.

Failure to praise would signal blindness or deafness. For our own sakes we must be alive to beauty and truth, and to give thanks for them. So today I call my heart, and yours as well, to awaken to gratitude. Without it we shall be blind and insensible and clueless. Paul was right on the mark, when, in his indictment of the pagan world, he listed a blind thanklessness as central to their ruin. Life is a gift. Wake up and see it; then let songs of joy break forth!

A New Beginning

Jeremiah 18:1-6

Isaac Newton once watched an apple fall to the ground in his garden. Suddenly, in that ordinary event, he was led to momentous new truth. Pondering why apples fall down,not up or out, or sideways, led Newton to formulate his famous laws of gravity and motion. Jeremiah too, found a new and powerful truth in a commonplace event:

The word that came to Jeremiah from the Lord: "Arise and go down to the potter's house, and there I will let you hear my words." So I went down to the potter's house, and there he was working at his wheel. And the vessel he was making of clay was spoiled in the potter's hand, and he reworked it into another vessel, as it seemed good to the potter to do. Then the word of the Lord came to me:

*"O house of Israel, can I not do with you as this potter
has done? Says the Lord. (Jer.18:1-6)*

The in-break of new truth came through a potter's accident. As he shaped a vessel of clay something went wrong. What
was the potter to do? Toss it into the trash? Discard it? No. He
smushed it into a fresh clump, put it on the spinning wheel, and
fashioned a new vessel. Like a flash came the word of God to the
prophet: *with God there can be new beginnings.*

This was not a lesson to be learned by just anyone visit-
ing a potter at work. Omar Khayyam too, went to a pottery once,
but where Jeremiah found a gospel of hope, Khayyam left with
gospel of despair. He thought of God as he watched the potter,
seeing him as an impassive, imperious maker who totally shapes
us however he will. An ice-cold, iron fatalism is at work in every
creature. How different from the gracious power revealed to Jeremiah. God never takes our marrings as final. He has the power
to remake us. Consider with me both the realism and the hope in
this word from long ago.

It says first that marring is an inescapable fact of life.
Know anyone who's escaped defeat and failure? Who's done it
all right? Even dressed in our Sunday best, when you pull back
the curtain, when you check the track record, you see flaws, mistakes, *cul de sacs* and yes, sins. That word has gone out of fash-
ion. Karl Menninger asked whatever became of sin in a book
with that title. There he documented the milder terms we use
to avoid the unwelcome word. We no longer lie, but rather mis-
speak or misstate. We prefer to ascribe any bad behavior to peer
pressure, being in the wrong crowd, or an error of judgment.
But when we are honest no euphemisms can disguise our lies,
infidelities and cruelties. Our lives are marred by betrayal, pride
and pettiness.

This happens in family life. Spouses, parents, children, siblings, all. There is none flawless, no not one. That's not how we planned it. We married with "sunny days and hopes up to the sky.," aspired to all the golden ideals: a love that deepens; healthy, supportive relationships; sensitive sharing and mutual growth. But we find, with a bleak monotony, the skulking shadows of failure. Emotional distance, estrangement and rebellion may replace our highest family hopes. We never planned the marring. It comes from our dreary bent to sinning.

It is no different in our workplaces. Where we want cooperation, respect, and fair treatment we see instead, jealousy, back-biting and malicious gossip. Ideals of camaraderie, honesty and fairness are surrendered to the pressures of our stumbling. In countless ways we do become marred vessels. When we flatly admit this, the good news of Jeremiah can shine like a light. Look!

The potter is persistent. He does not give up when the vessel is flawed. He works with determination and patient rescue. This is a picture of God's love which will not let us go. Despite any marring he sees worth and value. There is a mistaken stereotype of the Old Testament in which a God of law is stern and rather loveless, in contrast to a New Testament God who is loving and gracious. This passage in Jeremiah gives the lie to such a mistaken view. The gracious potter-God seeks to reclaim Israel despite her wayward flaws. The persistent potter just will not quit.

Jean Millet loved the peasants of Normandy and painted them in their toil and humble farm life. This was in a period when most artists preferred to paint the nobility: kings, queens, wealthy patrons. Millet's love and warm sympathy for these peasants allows us to see their dignity and worth.

Have your eyes ever been opened to unsuspected worth by someone who loved? In a village near a church I once served was a teenage boy who was running wild. He was getting drunk every weekend, racing at high speeds, endangering all around him. Then one Saturday night he plowed his speeding car into a telephone pole and died instantly. You could hear the comments all over the village: "Well I knew it was coming;" "You couldn't tell that boy nothin';" "Well that boy's dead, but we haven't lost much." But oh, if you could have heard his mother and father. Their grief was inconsolable. I thought of David's lament when he got the news of his son Absalom's death:

O my son Absalom, my son, my son Absalom! Would I had died instead of you, O Absalom, myson, my son. (II Sam 18: 33b)

There is a love that will not let us go! God's intolerable compliment is that he loves us too much to toss us away. A central part of Jesus' ministry was to the marred. Ask a jaded Samaritan woman with her unseemly bio, who found in him a frank but caring listener who awakened in her a thirst for living water. Or ask Zaccheus the tax collector, who, despite his handsome paycheck was a chronic out-cast in the worshipping community. Like the persistent potter, Jesus never quit on marred vessels. Jesus pressed for a meeting at his home, and in the triumph of grace could boldly announce, "Today salvation has come to this house."

There are those who insist that human nature can't change, but they underestimate the God of new beginnings. Louisa Tarkenton has a poem with these yearning words:

I wish there were some wonderful place
Called the Land of Beginning Again
Where all our mistakes, and all our heartaches
Could be dropped like a shabby old coat by the door.

I believe there is such a place, right in our midst: it is the workshop of our Potter-God How else could Paul, the fanatical persecutor—murderous, driven—become Paul the missionary-martyr for Christ?

There are many ways we need new beginnings. In his novel **The Fall**, Camus has a haunting passage about guilt. The lead character, a French lawyer, is remembering a night from years ago when he was young. Alone, in the darkness, he'd heard the cries of a young woman who had fallen into the river, but ignored her cries for help. Now, an old man, he says to himself, "And where were you that night on the quays of the Seine when you heard her screams and did nothing? O young woman, throw yourself again into the river, that I may save you and myself." Did you ever wish you could turn back the clock? Undo some shabby deed?

Khayyam believed in an irreversible fate:

The moving finger writes; and, having writ, moves on;
Nor all thy piety nor wit shall lure it back to cancel
half a line,
Nor all thy tears wash out a word of it.

Jeremiah knew better:

Can I not do with you as this potter has done? says the Lord.

Eldridge Cleaver learned it too. He became famous as a leader of the angry, militant Black Panthers. From prison he wrote his autobiography, **Soul on Ice**. After a shoot-out with Oakland police, he fled the country and found asylum in France. For a while in the 1960's and 1970's he was drawn to Marxism, but became disillusioned with it as just a new form of tyranny. His family life was not happy. He felt deep depression because his family wanted to return to the U.S. but his own criminal record made it impossible. Despondent, he went alone to their apartment on the Mediterranean near Cannes and began to think about putting an end to it by suicide. Sitting on the balcony of the thirteenth floor at night, even with the beauty of stars and a moonlit sky, he was brooding, downcast, at the end of his rope. As he gazed at the moon he kept seeing its shadows. First, he saw the man in the moon. Then he saw a profile of himself, like the one on Black Panther posters. Scared, he began to tremble. As he stared at the image it changed, and he started seeing faces of his old heroes. Fidel Castro, Mao Tse Tung, Karl Marx, Frederick Engels, passing in review. Finally, at the end of this procession, in dazzling light, the image of Jesus Christ appeared. Cleaver just crumbled and began to cry. Amid shaking and weeping he started to pray, and quote, as best he could, Bible passages he heard as a boy.

That night he slept the most peaceful sleep of his whole life, and he began to seriously seek to be a Christian. This story of new beginnings is told in the book he wrote called **Soul on Fire**. It shows the truth that Jeremiah learned. A soul on ice can be changed into a soul on fire by the power of God.

But there is a point at which the potter analogy breaks down. A lump of clay has no choice. The potter is in charge. But the remaking of any person is conditioned upon that person's willingness and inner consent. So the urgent question for every soul in desperate need of beginning again is the same question Jesus put to the infirm man beside the pool of Bethesda:

Wilt thou be made whole?

Well?

Interrupted by Praise

Romans 1:25; 9:1-5; 11: 33-36

When my wife was teaching the fifth grade she had a black student named Marsha who was deeply into jiving. Jiving was a form of rhythmic movements of the head, shoulders, arms and upper torso to the beat of some song playing within her head..Because this disrupted the class, my wife had made a strict rule: no jiving in class. One day during a test, as the students were bent over their work, she saw Marsha suddenly stop writing and doing a quick, impassioned jive. Just as suddenly she finished her jive, and resumed her writing. It was as if she could not contain the music within any longer, and it had to come out. She just could not keep the lid on something so good. I have come to believe that The Apostle Paul did something very like this three times in his letter to the Romans. Let me explain.

Paul customarily used a secretary to pen his letters. I am amazed at his felicity in dictation when I think of my own struggles with it. He was able to dictate complexities of sin and estrangement, of justification, of God's ultimate ploy to unite Jew and Gentile in glorious redemption. And he rattles this off as Tertius, his scribe, tries to keep up with pen and papyrus. A key reason for writing this letter was to summarize his approach and understanding of the gospel. If that important church concurred with his theology, he envisaged their endorsement and support of his missionary dream to take the gospel westward to Spain. So picture our Apostle, early in his exposition of his gospel, depicting the plight of the pagan world as it exchanges the truth of God—available to honest observation—for a lie. They worshipped creatures rather than the Creator—then Bang! His dictation was halted by that word "Creator," and he can't help himself: *"who is blessed forever! Amen."*(1:25) Paul's taxing, toilsome job of dictation was interrupted by praise. It will happen twice again.

Proceeding in his letter, Paul turns to a vexing circumstance that is a continual heartbreak for him. "Unceasing anguish," he calls it. The near-total rejection of Jesus as the Messiah by his kinsmen, the Jews, both baffles and devastates him. For their sake he could wish himself accursed. They had every opportunity; they had adoption, the Torah, the covenants, the glory, the promises; From them comes the Messiah—Boom! Again, a word triggers the interruption of praise: "who is over all, God blessed forever. Amen.(9:5)

Then back to his dictation. Amazingly, this "hardening" of the Jews is allowing you Gentiles to come in. Their disobedience, by the miracle of grace, invites the mercy of God for all –Bam! The in-break of praise once more: "O the depth of the riches and wisdom and knowledge of God! How unsearchable are his judgments and how inscrutable are his ways! For from him and through him and to him are all things. To him be the glory forever. Amen." (11:33; 36

These wondrous interruptions that come amid the tedious task of a lengthy transcription produce an admirable insight into Paul the man. He was indeed a new creation in Christ, where joy and gladness were easily at hand. The hardships of his work and mission could never silence or subdue his overriding cheer. I want for myself, and I want for you , fresh openings for the interruptions of praise all along our journeys. At the end of our puzzles and perplexities, beyond all of our anguish and tears, let praise and jubilant song abound. Like Bermuda grass pushing through the asphalt, I want praise to interrupt every difficulty.

Here, today, do you have any hurrahs or hallelujahs? Any deep gladness, or just grim, tight-lipped perseverance? Halford Luccock was impressed when he read that Eugene Ormandy, conductor of the Philadelphia orchestra, had dislocated his shoulder during a concert. He asked himself sadly, "Did I ever dislocate anything, even my necktie?"

Our threefold text from Paul's letter calls me to let praise interrupt everywhere. To awaken to gladness and the goodness of God's world. Edna St. Vincent Millay shows me the way in her response to the sudden beauty of an autumn tree:

O world, I cannot hold thee close enough!
Thy winds, thy wide gray skies!
Thy mists that roll and rise!
Thy woods, this autumn day, that ache and sag
And all but cry with color!

Lord I do fear
Thou'st made the world too beautiful this year.
My soul is all but out of me,--let fall
No burning leaf; prithee, let no bird call.

For Robert Frost it was an ordinary thing, but his antenna was up:

The way a crow shook down on me
The dust of snow from a hemlock tree

Has given my heart a change of mood
And saved some part of a day I had rued.

Frost's gift coaxes me to open my own eyes to wonder, and when I do, it calls me to thanksgiving. Not as a duty, but as the natural response to wondrous gifts. The great musicians help me. The powerful beauties of Vivaldi's *Gloria* are like fierce and lovely compressed springs; Handel's *Hallelujah Chorus* keeps driving, driving, fugue-like, to its glorious climax, while his *Thanks Be to Thee* simply melts the heart. Every Christmas season I listen once again to the Robert Shaw Chorale's *Adeste Fidelis* to interrupt my sometimes hectic holidays with glorious praise. I have an unforgettable memory of the Brigham Young Singers' concert, featured as a fundraiser for Public Television. As the college choir sang *Come, Thou Fount of Every Blessing,* the cameras panned the faces of the youthful singers. One lovely brunette co-ed caught my eye, for she was beautiful, as was the singing. As they sang the third verse, the camera was right on her when they came to the words, *"prone to wander, Lord I feel it, prone to leave the God I love."* I watched as a tear ran down her cheek, and as we both pondered our proneness to wander, a tear ran down mine as well. But because that hymn celebrates the grace of God which so completely surrounds us, it was still a bright interruption of praise.

I want, above all things, to avoid falling victim to the "blahs" or that strange spiritual amnesia of forgetting that I have been purged from my old sins. I want to keep vivid the joy of having found a pearl of great price; the exhilaration of stumbling upon a hidden treasure in a field. I would like my journey to be surprisingly waylaid by doxology and praise time and time again. This can happen even in the shadows and the hard times. Remember, Paul and Silas sang in jail. Samuel Rutherford reported that Christ came to him in his prison cell and every stone flashed like a ruby. My friend, a fellow minister, developed cancer as a young man with school children still at home. He went to a Chattanooga hospital to learn the results of diagnostic tests he had taken about the suspected cancer. They proved to be positive, and as he was leaving the hospital with the dreaded news, he walked down the front steps holding the test results in an attache case he carried. Overwhelmed and angry, he raised his eyes to the sky, flung his brief case high in the air and shouted, "Whatta ya think you're doing?!" The case popped open, and papers were scattered everywhere. An elderly black man began to help pick up the papers, saying to him, "It's gonna be all right." Shortly afterward my friend was called to another church 150 miles away. I kept in contact through his church newsletter, which I received week by week. I shall never forget what he wrote in one of those newsletters. He began by quoting Psalm 134: *"Come, bless the Lord, all you servants of the Lord, who stand by night in the house of the Lord."* Then he said, "I myself am standing by night in the house of the Lord. My illness makes it night time, but God gives me strength to stand in his house and bless his name."

For me, his courage and honesty remain to lift my soul with the interruption of praise—even in the shadows. It was, and is, a song in the night.

John Claypool, a pastor who delivered the Beecher Lectures on Preaching at Yale in 1979, endured the fierce assault of darkness when his eight-year-old daughter, Laura Lue, was diagnosed with acute leukemia. They did everything they could, medically, and she fought bravely, but she died a year and a half later on a snowy Saturday night. Claypool spent a month in grief work away from his pulpit. His first sermon after the family's loss was a searching, honest treatment of what he learned in the Darkness. Admitting freely to the shock and painful questions her death had triggered, he believed his best response was to see life as a gift, and used an old childhood memory to illustrate his point. He was a child during World War II. A young man who worked with his father was drafted into military service. Because his wife was going with him, they stored their furniture in the Claypool's basement, and suggested that they use their washing machine since the Claypool's did not have one. Young John, who helped with the family's washing, loved the help the green Bendix provided. By the time the war ended he had forgotten how the washer had come to be in their basement anyway. When they came and got the washer the boy was terribly upset and said so openly. But his mother sat him down to put things in perspective for him. "Wait a minute, son. You must remember that the washer never belonged to us in the first place. That we ever got to use it at all was a gift. So, instead of being mad that it's gone, let's use this occasion to be grateful that we had it at all." From that story, he moved to Laura Lue. "It makes things bearable when I remember that Laura Lue was a gift, pure and simple, something I neither earned nor deserved nor had a right to. And when I remember that the appropriate response to a gift, even when it is taken away, is gratitude, then I am better able to try and thank God that I was ever given her in the first place." This insightful, articulate preacher shows me that even our profoundest suffering can be interrupted by praise.

So, wherever you are, whatever your pathway, be alert for the forays of doxology. In the darkness of grief keep your antenna up. In the gray hum-drum, in the monotony of days without lift or lilt, who knows? Maybe praise lies hidden somewhere. Let it break in!

Heaven's Gate Was Open Wide

Matthew 23:37

It is true that some of God's blessings come to everyone regardless. You do nothing to earn the sunshine or rain: He makes his sun to rise on the evil and the good, and sends rain upon the just and the unjust. (Mt.5:45) God's best blessings, however, come only by our choosing. Jesus, near the end of his ministry, wept over the plight of Jerusalem.

Only twice in all the Gospel records are we told that he wept. Once, over a dead friend; now over a dead city. The words of his lament have a deep and haunting pathos. Cool prophetic realism joins a poignant tenderness: *O Jerusalem, Jerusalem, killing the prophets and stoning those who are sent to you! How often would I have gathered your children together as a hen gathers her brood under her wings, and you would not!*(Mt.23:37)

This text is the tale of two wills: Jesus' longing for Jerusalem's high blessing, and the city's stony refusal. I know of no doctrine of predestination that spans the distance between Jesus' "I would" and Jerusalem's "would not." Jesus, in rapport with the freedom of human choice, can only add, with choked voice, "Behold, your house is forsaken and desolate."

Years ago, in the church I attended in my college days, I heard Dr. J.Winston Pearce quote a bit of poetry that fits this situation precisely:

> *Heaven's gate was open wide;*
> *still the gypsies camped outside.*

The tragedy of the gypsies is a nomadic life-style that deprives them of the rewards of settled life: homes, utilities, steady jobs, schools and hospitals. God's best and highest blessings can be won only by our choosing, or lost by our own refusal.

Jesus once visited the land of the Gadarenes in the Decapolis. In a dramatic miracle of exorcism he brought peace and sanity to tormented Legion. This madman who cried out and cut himself with sharp stones, who snapped the ropes of every attempt to confine him, was made whole by Jesus. When the townspeople got the word and came to see, they found Legion sitting at Jesus' feet, clothed and in his right mind. Gripped by a kind of terror, the crowd begged Jesus to leave their region. He did not argue, he did not scold. He just climbed into his boat and sailed out of their lives. Heaven's gate was open wide. . .

All through the Bible's pages momentous choices are given: Eden or eviction; life or death; curse or blessing; mending nets or seeking the kingdom. I want to sketch out potential blessings that are offered to all in our time.

The first is *God's Guidance*. In choosing our life-journeys we may be the drifters, the driven, or the led. Drifters have few goals or passions. They mostly bob along through life, passive playthings of winds and waves. The driven, however, have plenty of goals. They may be high , lofty goals, but can also be unworthy: pride, envy, lust or greed. The led choose the guidance of God as their pilot. They claim the proffered security of

Psalm 23: *"The Lord is my shepherd."* Living as we all do, suspended daily over doubt and brokenness, facing baffling forks in the road, God's guidance is a priceless thing.

Ernie Pyle was a brave war correspondent in the Second World War, but had not chosen God's guidance. In his gutsy choice of reporting the war from its gory, wrenching front lines, he wrote a minister friend: "It seems to me that living is futile and death is the final indignity." Later, he wrote him again in deeper desperation, "If you have any light, please shine it in my direction. God knows I've run out of light." The God who guides us does not offer unruffled calm, but he does offer a pathway lit up with meaning and a peace that passes all understanding. It is ours—for the taking: *Heaven's gate is open wide . . .*

The second is *Help in Trial and Storm*. As the winds of life beat, no one is untouched by their surges. hurricanes assault our marriages; high winds shake our work and our families. And fierce hidden storms may rage inside us, hidden in the shadows. I'm not sure what storm exactly Oscar Wilde was battling, but I hear the desperation in his cry:

> *Come down, O Christ, and help me! Reach thy hand,*
> *For I am drowning in a stormier sea*
> *Than Simon on thy lake of Galilee:*

The gift offered to us by God is not a storm-free haven, but dependable help in weathering all storms. This cannot be said too often, because our air waves and bookstores are overrun with gospel peddlers who promise health, wealth and phony security as shiny perks for prospective converts. If I read Scripture aright, to choose God's way is to actually invite some storms: *If any man would come after me, let him deny himself and take up his cross . . . !*

Paul told the Ephesian elders, as he set his face for Jerusalem's powder keg, *"I am going , not knowing what shall befall me, except that the Holy Spirit testifies to me that imprisonment and afflictions await me."* The offered gift, then, is not immunity from trouble, but God's unfailing presence amid the tumult. This may seem scant comfort for seekers of a safer hothouse discipleship, but trusting veterans of the cross are well-acquainted with the compensations of God's leading:

When you pass through the waters I will be with you; and through the rivers, they shall not overwhelm you; when you walk through the fire you shall not be burned, and the flame shall not consume you...I will make a way in the wilderness and rivers in the desert. (Is.43:2;19b)

The third is *Christ as Savior.* The last crucial choice I will discuss is the most urgent of all. The New Testament is brimming with breathless good news of God's saving work in Christ. Through him comes the gift with countless names: salvation, light, life, forgiveness, reconciliation, adoption---Where shall we stop? Through Christ the Son, God has opened heaven's gate to the whole creation. Like any invitation, it may be declined or accepted. Our choosing is the pivotal point.

Wordsworth has a pastoral poem about Michael, a shepherd in England's Lake Country. Michael and his wife had a son when she was almost past the age of child-bearing. Luke was the name they gave him. Old Michael was fully 20 years older than his wife, and having a child in his old age gave him the precious gifts of hope and new, forward-looking thoughts. A rare and inseparable bond of love developed between the two. The boy went everywhere with Michael, who made a shepherd's staff for him when he turned five. Together, every day, year after year, they worked the sheep.

When Luke was eighteen years old distressing word came to their family. Years before Michael had guaranteed a loan for his brother's son. Unforeseen misfortune in the nephew's finances now meant that the debt became Michael's own. The only solution, it seemed, was for Michael to sell a part of his beloved pasture land. But the thought of selling half his land— land his father had worked and that he fondly planned to leave to Luke—made his heart sink. They decided that Luke would go off to work for a prosperous kinsman long enough to pay off the debt.. Then Luke could return and possess the fields that he and his father so deeply loved.

On the evening before Luke's leaving for the distant city, old Michael took him out to the field to a heap of stones he had been piling up near a brook. His plan was for a sheepfold. "This was a work for both of us; and now, my son, it is a work for me. But lay one stone with your own hands-- it will be a covenant between us. I'll work here while you work in the city, and when you return it will be to claim this land of my family for your own."

Luke left the next day; good reports of his work came from the city kinsman. Warm letters came from Luke; and Michael worked on the sheepfold at every chance. But after many months Luke's letters stopped. He began to run with a lowlife crowd, gave in to evil ways, and finally fled into hiding somewhere across the seas.

Old Michael kept going, they say, to the sheepfold brook, but "many and many a day he thither went, and never lifted a single stone."He would sit there alone , or with his faithful dog. He died a few years later, and in three years his wife died as well. The land was sold into a stranger's hand, and the remains of a half-built sheepfold can still be seen. It is a story of a father's hopes and a son's refusal. Heaven's gate was open wide.

God offers to all the highest gift of all: Christ as Savior. It would seem an obvious choice to make, a no-brainer as we say. But yet there is a strange reluctance, a dread almost, of being chosen. Augustine knew the dread: "It was I who willed, I who nilled." Paul Tillich said, "A man who has never tried to flee God has never experienced the God who is really God." No wonder that even standing before a wide-open gate, old gypsies feel the stubborn pull of their wandering ways. And no wonder proud Jerusalem, disdaining Jesus' tender overtures, headed on to ruin.

But still the seeking Christ stands at the open gate, inviting all to life, and all of heaven cries, "Come!"

Living in the Red

Matthew 10:8b

As Matthew tells the story of Jesus sending out the Twelve we learn that it will involve preaching the good news that the kingdom of heaven was at hand. They were to heal the sick, cleanse the lepers, raise the dead, and cast out demons. Jesus then gave them the motive and watchword of their mission: "Freely you have received, freely give." As they head out on this compassionate mission of proclamation and   blessing they must keep in mind that they themselves had been recipients of grace before they were sharers of grace. What had they received? Jesus Christ, the unspeakable gift! They had been given an outright gift of grace freely, and now they freely pass it on. On this day of our church homecoming we are called to a similar mission. All of our call to mission rests in the conviction that we are debtors to grace. Think with me as we ponder the first half of our watchword text: Freely you have received.

Paul Scherer had a way of saying, "I've always lived my life in the red: hopelessly indebted to others who have given so much. Our lives and our achievements are not entirely ours alone. Samuel Proctor said when you find a turtle on a stump you know one thing: it didn't get there by itself. We have all met those arrogant types who boast that they are self-made men. I heard of one whose character was so coarse and unseemly, that when he made that ridiculous claim a man who knew him well said, " believe I'da called in some help." None of us are self-made men or women. We all stand on the shoulders of giants. Let this very sanctuary where celebrate homecoming be a symbol of our indebtedness. Did you build this building? Did you write the hymns we sing? Did you compose the music, or translate the Bible in your pew rack?

We thank God for a whole cloud of witnesses before our time who have enriched our lives with countless gifts of love. I like to call them my unseen benefactors. To study the Bible, or to study church history, is to learn how my faith was formed and reformed by those marvelous benefactors. It widens your world. I once read in some forgotten book of Edith. The one passage I remember went like this:"Edith lived in a small world bounded on the north, south, east and west by Edith." The Lord delivered me from such foolish blinders through great Christian writers.

I cannot calculate the debt I owe to Augustine, Kierkegaard, or Reinhold Niebuhr. I have loved reading C.S. Lewis, C.H. Dodd, and Robert Frost. Freely I have received from Flannery O'Connor, William Hull and L.D. Johnson. My preaching, indeed my grasp of the gospel itself, has been enriched beyond all telling by John Claypool and George Truett, by Paul Scherer and George Buttrick. Freely have I received from Fred Craddock and Ernest Campbell. Here, now, I raise my Ebenezer for their golden gifts.

I have spoken of those who blessed my life by books and study, but I have a whole cavalcade of ordinary saints that I actually knew to whom I am in debt. I think of my mother who taught me prayer. I think of my father, Who taught me honesty and hard work. These words may sound trite, but we live in an alarming culture where countless couples procreate routinely with no thought of parental duty to guide and mentor their all-too-casual progeny. Our faith is neither self-generated nor self-sustained. So today I honor my father and mother, not least for showing me the way morally and spiritually.

I'm hopelessly in debt to teachers along my way. Like Mrs. Shirah, who through her flannelgraph stories instilled a love for Scripture; like Dr. Hill, who showed me the thrill of contending theologies; or like Dr. Hull, who embodied the votive offering to God of one's finest gifts of mind. Oh, yes, I'm living totally in the red. My 80 years reveal a long procession of ordinary saints who have enriched me beyond all telling. They have, at times, come as desperately needed help.

During my seminary training I experienced a period when all my foundations were shaking. I felt fear and deep depression, and questioned my faith and my calling. But I discovered a lifeline. About two years earlier I had served as youth minister for a summer before starting seminary. Upon finishing that summer job, I was presented a gift of two books: **Cruden's Concordance** and **Smith's Bible Dictionary**. In my crisis of faith I remembered the gracious inscriptions of those books:

Presented to Dan by the Married Young People, First Baptist Church, Titusville, in appreciation of his devotion and untiring efforts in promoting interest in the program of the young people of the church during the summer of 1960.

Those treasured words in the inscriptions I read and reread in my down times. They provided affirmation and assurance for me in a time when God himself seemed silent. Freely, freely I have received.

John Bunyan points the way to genuine thanks for people along his pathway who blessed his life and nudged him

Godward. In his book **Grace Abounding to the Chief of Sinners,** he wrote that when he married, it was "my mercy to light upon a wife whose father was counted godly. This woman and I, though we came together as poor as poor might be, not having so much household stuff as a dish or spoon between us both, yet this she had for her part, '**The Plain Man's Pathway to Heaven'** and '**The Practice of Piety,**' which her father had left her when he died." Those books were the beginning of God's calling of grace.

He has a way of placing people along our pathway who wield crucial influence. For example, my seminary room mate, Will Manley, had been a Marine recruit, cocky and savvy in the ways of the rough-and-tumble world. He did not appear to be a promising candidate for Christianity, let alone ministry. But a Marine buddy of Will's—Shaky Davis—made the difference. Shaky—who got his nickname because of his extreme shyness and nervous temperament-- had the courage to invite Will to his church's Brotherhood supper. There Will met accepting, warm Christian friends and a pastor who cared. He began to attend this church, was led to conversion and committed his life to the ministry. Shaky Davis was an unlikely witness, but became a stepping-stone to God for Will.

Every Christian I know has had their own personal stepping-stones to God. So let me propose for all of us an informal, but wholesome liturgy: throughout the course of our days, without naming them canonical hours like lauds or vespers, find time to whisper, "Freely I have received."

But it is urgent, as well, to whisper the second half of our watchword: "Freely give." The endless stream of blessings we have received demand from us the ministry of giving back. Not all can see this. Once, as I was on a street in Macon, Georgia, I saw a car with a bold message lettered across the rear window. It seemed to me that it had an "attitude:"Don't O U Nothin'" Pity the driver so blind to what he had freely received in his young life.

It was far different with Albert Schweitzer. As a gifted organist, holder of doctorates in philosophy and theology, his life turned in a new direction at the age of thirty. He had seen an article in a Paris missionary society magazine entitled *"The Needs of the Congo Mission."* It was an appeal for someone to offer himself for work in Africa. Knowing of the desperate need for medical help, he decided to study medicine. This required seven years of intensive study.

This costly choice was rooted in a crucial experience he had at the age of twenty-one. He was in Gunsbach, where his father was pastor of a little flock of evangelical Christians. He awakened on a brilliant summer morning when his world seemed full of happiness. "There came to me as I awoke," Schweitzer later wrote, "the thought that I must not accept this happiness as a matter of course but must give something in return for it." He decided there in bed that he could justify pursuing music and his studies until he was thirty, and then would give himself completely to the direct service of humanity.

Sadly, most of his friends tried to talk him out of what they saw as the folly of his plan. "In the many verbal duels which I had to fight," he later wrote, "as a weary opponent with people who passed for Christians, it moved me strangely to see them so far from perceiving that the love preached by Jesus may sweep a man into a new course of life." Like Paul before him, Schweitzer felt himself a debtor. Both of them were convinced they were living in the red, and the only proper response was to pass on the grace they had so fully received. One of the treasured quotations I cherish most from my seminary classrooms came from Dr. Olin Binkley: "In the light of what God has done for me through Jesus Christ, what ought I to think, and say, and do in the concrete situations of life?"

In a world of grabbers we are called to become givers. We are not self-made. "Freely we all have received." Mark Hopkins was the President of Williams College when a student from a wealthy family defaced some property on campus. He was called to the President's office to face the music. When confronted with the damage he had done, he casually pulled out his wallet and asked how much he owed. Hopkins angrily ordered him to sit down. "No man can pay for what he receives here," he said. "Can you pay for the sacrifices of Col. Williams who founded this school? Can you pay for those half-paid professors who remained here to teach when they could have gone elsewhere? Every student in this school is a charity case!"

And so are we all. The countless gifts of love, the benefactions of parents, teachers,friends, the grace of God in Christ, all saddle us with a debt. We are living in the red. Surrounded by a world of pain and need, of desolate spiritual ruin, our only joy, our only salvation is "freely give!"

Our Pain as God's Grace

Luke 15: 11-32

The parable of the prodigal son is, I believe, the best-known, best-loved of all the parables of Jesus. It is like a cut and polished gem, which held up and turned to the light, reveals many wondrous facets. For example, it pictures God as a waiting father. When the boy returned home, while he was still a long way off, his father ran to meet him. How many times had this father stood and looked down the road, waiting, waiting, in endless love? Or turn it to another facet. The new robe, the ring, the sandals, the fatted calf—these point us to heaven's joy at a sinner's return.

Still, again, it depicts sin as rebellion, as the squandering of God's gifts. But allow me to focus on yet another facet: our pain as a gracious gift of God. It was pain that turned the wayward boy homeward. After the fun of partying, after the big spending spree in the far country, he was broke and in want. There was famine in the land, and famine in his purse. He is reduced to taking a job tending the hogs. Hungry amid the rooting swine, he would have gladly fed on the husks they ate. It was in the pain and misery of his situation that "he came to himself." He decided to head home and ask to become a servant.

God used pain as a means of grace and rescue. C.S. Lewis said it well: "God whispers in our pleasure, shouts in our pain. It is God's megaphone to rouse a deaf world." We don't usually think this way. We think pain is bad, pleasure is good. But John Newton too, found in his own experience that the seeking God will find odd ways to reach us: "Twas grace that taught my heart to fear, and grace my fears relieved." It reveals God's humility to reach us through pain or fear. He wants us even when we've shown that we prefer everything else to him. He will use the side door He stoops to conquer. In the case of the Prodigal, God used pain as a spur to health and wholeness.

Let's examine three ways God uses pain as a form of grace. First, *Salvation*. John Bunyan wrote a book describing how God saved him: **Grace Abounding to the Chief of Sinners.** He was born of humble parents who were not especially religious, but did send him to school where he learned to read and write. When he married, he wrote, "It was my mercy to light upon a wife whose father was counted godly." He had died, and left to her two books: **The Plain Man's Pathway to Heaven**, and **The Practice of Piety.** Reading in the books awakened some interest in religion for Bunyan.

One day, while plying his trade as a tinker in Bedford, he overheard three or four poor women sitting at a door in the sun, talking about the things of God. He drew nearer to hear what they said. But though he heard, he did not understand, for they were far above his reach. Their talk was of a new birth; of God's work in their hearts; of how their souls had been refreshed and comforted. "And methought they spoke as if joy did make them speak." He left them, but their talk went with him. He left greatly moved.

Memories of the happiness of those poor women soon were presented to him as a kind of vision. He saw them sitting on the side of some high mountain, refreshing themselves with the pleasant beams of the sun, while he was shivering in the cold, frosty dark side of the mountain. What he felt was psychic pain, misery of the spirit. But the pain was God's grace at work, for it called him to joyous salvation.

In his Confessions, Augustine wrote of this same truth: "Thou hast made us for thyself, and our heart is restless until it finds its rest in Thee." I think of Francis Thompson, both brilliant and a basket case. His father was a physician and wanted his son to follow in his steps. He took the medical course, but had no interest it. He failed at a succession of jobs: book agent, bootmaker, soldier. He decided to go to London, not so much to seek his fortune as to escape his misfortune. There he sold matches, ran errands, held horses' heads and became a laudanum addict. Wilfred and Alice Meynell, a Christian couple of literary note, discovered his poetic gift and took him in to their home.

There he wrote, besides many other poems, *The Hound of Heaven*. It is a marvelous ode that has captured more readers than any other religious poem. The poem pictures God as the hound of heaven, in pursuit of Thompson himself:

> *I fled Him, down the nights and down the days;*
> *I fled Him, down the arches of the years;*
> *I fled Him down the labyrinthine ways*
> *Of my own mind; and in the mist of tears*
> *I hid from Him . . .*

Thompson tells in the poem of the countless ways he sought to find happiness, but how, no matter what he tried, he found only ashes: he hears God's stern rebukes: *"All things betray thee, who betrayest Me. Naught shelters thee, who wilt not shelter Me. Naught contents thee, who content'st not Me."* Thompson's painful search for joy and meaning was God in gracious pursuit, intending that he turn to the true source of salvation and joy:

All which I took from thee I did but take,
    Not for thy harms,
But just that thou might'st seek it in my arms.
    All which thy child's mistake
Fancies as lost, I have stored for thee at home:
    Rise, clasp my hand, and come!

Pain is clearly used by God as a severe mercy to accomplish our salvation.

Second, God uses *Christian Growth*. Christians are new creations in Christ to be sure, but the transforming work is not complete. Over and over we must "put to death the old man with his deeds." Those vestiges of our old selves include anger, wrath, malice, slander, and greed. Each of these traits creates havoc in our relationships. They rip the fabric of community, and in so doing they bring pain. They bring pain not only to the victims of such vices, but to the perpetrators as well. An angry person is often lonely, for example,because people avoid him. To get too close is like getting too near a porcupine: you could get yourself quilled. Therefore, loneliness is painful. I believe God seeks for the pain of it to prompt change and growth in us—to induce putting off the "old man."

I had a college roommate who has been a lifelong friend. His college years were rough. First, he entered his freshman year just after being jilted by his fiancee. He had been stationed in Europe by the Air Force, carrying on his romance with a girl back home through letters. Their love deepened, and the engagement was made from across the Atlantic. He ended his military hitch and returned home about a month before the wedding date. Sadly, the face-to-face romance was far rockier than the postal courtship, and she called the wedding off. Right away it was time to enter college. As his roommate I met a man deeply depressed. I learned also that my new friend as a teenager had to physically step in to protect his mother from attack by his father, who had developed a very serious mental illness and soon was sent to the state mental hospital.

You must try to picture my freshman roommate: recently jilted; his family in crisis; and then new trouble: his grades were deficient in several courses. In fact, he stayed on academic probation all four years of his college career. In order to graduate he had to make a B in a certain final semester class. I can still remember hearing his victorious whoop when he learned he made the B and would indeed graduate with us.

Naturally my friend developed anger issues. He locked horns with faculty, with students, and with townspeople too. His many stresses fostered deep anger, and that same anger followed him to seminary; to his first pastorate (where he was fired), and to his marriage (his wife divorced him). Through all those pain-filled events I tried to be a sympathetic friend, a listening ear. Years later, upon being fired after an angry confrontation with his supervisor at the post office, he called me on the phone to report his latest trouble. I decided to do something I had never done before. In place of my usual attempts to hear him without really confronting his pattern of anger, I decided to talk straight with my friend. I wrote him a long letter and told him his anger was a large part of his many conflicts. I was aware of some of the sources of his anger, I told him, but I believed his anger was often a defense against hurt. I suggested he meet with a trusted counselor to help find new ways of coping. I feared that my new-found candor would cause more anger and defensiveness, and maybe even end our friendship, but mercifully, he was able to accept my suggestion and found help in "putting away anger." I believe pain was God's megaphone to get his attention and enable Christian growth.

Third, God uses *Desert Places*. As a young minister, Dr. Harry Emerson Fosdick experienced a critical nervous breakdown. It was frightening and painful, but as he later said, "I found God in a desert." From his struggles in those dark hours came his book, **The Meaning of Prayer**, a gift of light and help to many thousands of readers. His suffering, like that of Job, the prophet Jeremiah, and the apostle Paul, has been a channel of God's help and comfort to the weary and heavy-laden. Pain is an improbable, but effective, tutor:

I walked a mile with pleasure; she chatted all the way;
But I was none the wiser for all she had to say.
I walked a mile with sorrow, and ne'er a word said she;
But O, the things I learned from her, when sorrow
walked with me.

The desert places of our lives, for all their anguish, can prove to become oases for unexpected grace. George Matheson, a Scottish minister, suffered poor eyesight from birth, and at age 15 learned he was going blind. Feeling called to Christian ministry, he enrolled in the University of Glasgow, and graduated at age 19. When he began theological studies it was then that he became totally blind. His three sisters became his tutor. They learned enough Latin, Greek and Hebrew to get him through. After graduation he was called to the church in Innellan. On the day of his sister's wedding, with all his family gathered in Glasgow, he remained at the manse in Innellan, and wrote a hymn. He tells in his journal how it happened:

My hymn was composed in the manse of Innellan on the
evening of June 6, 1882. I was at that time alone. It was
the day of my sister's marriage, and the rest of the family
were staying overnight in Glasgow. Something had hap-
pened to me which was known only to myself, and which
caused me the most severe mental suffering. The hymn
was the fruit of that suffering.

The hymn is *O Love That Wilt Not Let Me Go*, and is a testimony to God's grace, in which pain had been the catalyst.

Matheson's secret pain almost certainly was a heart-breaking experience a few years earlier. His fiancee had broken her engagement to him, telling him that she couldn't see herself going through life married to a blind man. He never married, and it seems that his sister's wedding must have been a pain-filled reminder of the love he had lost. Do not the words of his hymn speak powerfully to pain's role as an impetus to new-found grace?

O Love that wilt not let me go, I rest my weary soul in Thee;
I give Thee back the life I owe,
That in Thine ocean depths its flow
May richer, fuller be.

O Light that foll'west all my way,
I yield my flick'ring torch to Thee;
My heart restores its borrowed ray,
That in Thy sunshine's glow its day
May brighter, fairer be.

O Joy that seekest me thro' pain,
I cannot close my heart to Thee;
I trace the rainbow thro' the rain,
And feel the promise is not vain
That morn shall tearless be.

O Cross that liftest up my head,
I dare not ask to hide from Thee;
I lay in dust life's glory dead,
And from the ground there blossoms red,
Life that shall endless be.

We have looked at several different ways where pain can be a doorway to God"s grace. It means that the Hound of Heaven will stop at nothing to catch us. His seeking grace leaves us no place to flee or hide. C.S. Lewis put it with his usual verve and point: "A young man who wishes to remain a sound atheist cannot be too careful of his reading. There are traps everywhere—'Bibles laid open, millions of surprises,' as Herbert says, 'fine nets and stratagems.' God is, if I may say it, very unscrupulous."

So you there: are you experiencing some kind of pain? What may God be saying to you? It just might be some hidden grace.

She Has Done What She Could

Mark 14: 3-9

Jesus' prediction has come true: wherever the good news is proclaimed in the whole world, what she has done for me will be told in remembrance of her. Here, in a small Georgia town nearly two thousand years later my sermon centers upon her beautiful act.

In Bethany, near the end, as chief priests and scribes plot his ruin, as Judas conspires in grim betrayal, as the darkness closes in, this nameless woman anointed his head with costly perfume. It was at the home of Simon the leper who was hosting a meal. Some at the meal were angry at the woman.

Why was the ointment wasted this way? It could have been sold for a small fortune, and the money given to the poor." But Jesus came to her defense with words of deep approval. "Why do you trouble her? She has done a beautiful thing for me." Then he adds, in low-key, genuine appreciation, "She has done what she could."

This simple phrase is an excellent foundation for how we may respond to tangled, complex situations. There was much she could not do. She could not halt the plot to kill him; she could not undo the hatred; she could not rescue him from entrenched systems of power. Yet she did not let the impossibilities rob her of the possibilities. If she could not prevent his death, she could affirm her love.

Now leave Bethany and Simon's home, and come to where we live. Worldwide news media report to us daily about massive geo-political problems. Famine, war, drug traffic, sex traffic and genocide bombard our ears and eyes with a hateful monotony. In our own personal lives, and the lives of our families, we meet tangled problems that seem to defy solution. The lesson from Bethany is (1) *you can't do everything*, but (2) *you can do something*. Let's explore this response that Jesus commended.

Avoiding Grandiosity. I often overestimate my power and ability as a minister. Like old Elijah, I am tempted to think God's cause is riding on me. I well remember a telling event in my youthful ministry. I grew up in the segregated South, but came to see how wrong it was in my seminary training. So in my first pastorate after seminary I accepted chairmanship of our Baptist Association's committee for work with National Baptists (Negro). Our committee recommended that we observe a Sunday of pulpit exchange between our two groups. As chairman I urged white pastors by word and letters to participate.

But it was 1972, and the civil rights movement had sparked tension and massive resistance. I knew full well that my own church was divided on my proposal. Several days before my own church conference was to meet and vote on whether or not to participate, I called a close friend and fellow pastor. I was worried, I told him , because I had earnestly pressed my fellow pastors to take part in the pulpit exchange, but feared the embarrassment if my own church refused. I will never forget the simple wisdom of my friend's response. "You have done what you could. If they refuse, it is their decision not yours." He was speaking to my grandiosity; to my frantic, anxious activism; to my mistaken view that I must solve all, save all.

A sense of guilt should be my best clue . It is the guilt of omnipotence if I expect perfect power or total control. If my children are not happy, I cannot assume the blame. Have I done what I could? The angels in heaven can't do more.A minister once talked to an older veteran pastor about his difficulties with two or three of his church members. He was sure he had failed in his leadership. "Who told you that you could pastor everybody?" was his friend's insightful question. He might have added another question: "Who told you that you could win them all?"

When Jesus sent out the Twelve on a mission to the cities of Israel, he gave them what John Oman called a sacrament of failure. *"If anyone will not welcome you or listen to your words, shake off the dust of your feet as you leave that house or town."* This was not a gesture of anger , but a recognition that the call of other towns outweighs an obsessive need to succeed. You have done what you could.

But I see more in Jesus' warm approval of the Bethany woman more than a warning against grandiosity. It was also a check on our inertia. If she could not do everything she could do something. When we are overwhelmed by massive needs we can never fully meet, we still must not surrender to doing nothing. I read of a man in New York who was bothered by the trash and litter all about him. He knew he could not solve the problem totally, but he decided to pick up three or four pieces of trash every day. This was his simple refusal to yield to doing nothing if he could not do everything.

You can't possibly teach every child to know and love Christ, but you could teach one class of children. All four gospels record the miraculous feeding of thousands when five loaves and two fish were given to Jesus and blessed by him. Our skimpy efforts at a thousand things can be multiplied for more good than we know when perfect solutions are not possible. "She has done what she could." Is this something of what William James meant when he wrote,

> I am done with great things and big things, with great institutions and big success, and I am for those tiny, invisible molecular forces, that work from individual to individual, creeping through the crannies of the world like so many soft rootlets, or like the capillary oozing of water, but which, give them time, will rend the hardest monuments of men's pride.

Christian thinkers of the Middle Ages named sloth as one of seven deadly sins. They meant, of course, more than laziness. Sloth is a spirit of dejection, a sense of futility that gives rise to a morbid kind of inertia. Sloth cares for nothing, believes nothing, attempts nothing. Greek mythology told of Sisyphus, the king of Corinth, was punished in Hades by being forced to roll a huge stone up a hill every day, only to have it roll back down as soon as he reached the top. It is the perfect image of futility. I like to imagine that Paul, when writing to a church in Corinth— the very town Sisyphus ruled, just might have been playing on that old tale of futility when he wrote, *"be steadfast,immovable, always excelling in the work of the Lord, because you know that in the Lord your labor is not in vain."* (I Cor.15: 58) Whenever we do what we can, the humblest labor is not in vain.

Let me in closing go back to Bethany where we began. An unnamed woman at Simon's home broke her jar of treasured perfume and poured it all on Jesus' head. When her stingy critics objected Jesus said, "Leave her alone. She has done a beautiful thing for me. She has done what she could. She has anointed my body beforehand for its burial." As best I can tell this happened less than a week before his crucifixion. How long would the fragrance of her extravagant effusion last? I don't believe it is hard to imagine that the scent of the love-gift nard that had drenched his hair and upper body persisted even as he hung on his cross. Maybe, just maybe it interrupted the harsh derision of the carnival crowd with the memory of a woman who had done what she could that day in Bethany.

Paul and the Wastebasket

Philippians 3:8-14

Paul is a hero of mine, and I am drawn to him in count-less ways. I admire his gift for deep friendships. The remarkable success of his ministry to the Gentiles owes much to his choice of fellow workers. His wide net of friendship held Barnabas, Silas, Luke, Priscilla and Acquila, Timothy, Titus, to name but a few. Also I admire his way with words. Who could ever for-get his flashes of eloquence: the ode to agape (I Cor.13); his hymn-like meters in the kenosis passage in Philippians 2; or his fugue-like plaudits to Christ in the opening of Colossians? Think also of Paul's remarkable bond of love for the churches. Think of his magnificent obsession with Christ.

This hero of mine gives us another clue to his greatness in the text I have chosen. It is a biographical passage that tells us one of the secrets to his greatness:

Indeed I count everything as loss for the sake of Christ.
For his sake I have suffered the loss of all things, and

*I count them as refuse, in order that I may gain Christ
and be found in him, not having a righteousness of my
own, based on law, but that which is through faith in
Christ, the righteousness of God that depends on faith.
That I may know him and the power of his resurrection,
and may share his sufferings, becoming like him in his
death, that if possible I may attain the resurrection from
the dead. Not that I have already attained this or am already perfect; but I press on to make it my own, because
Christ Jesus has made me his own. Brethren, I do not
consider that I have made it my own; but one thing I
do, forgetting what lies behind and straining forward to
what lies ahead, I press on toward the goal for the prize
of the upward call of God in Christ Jesus.* (Phil. 3: 8-14)

The text is Paul's account of his necessary losses in becoming a follower of Christ. He lost his old approach to God,
his stringent effort to please God by keeping the law. He seems
to have kept a sort of   trophy case of achievement in keeping
the law of God. He had out-Phariseed the other Pharisees in his
own estimation. He aspired to be a Prometheus of the Torah. But
when he met the risen Christ he felt forced to relinquish his pride
and drivenness. The new Paul found a new obsession: a holy
quest to gain Christ in all his fulness; to know him in the power
of his resurrection and the fellowship of his suffering. This goal
was not yet reached. But then Paul shares a secret of his greatness: *"But one thing I do, forgetting what lies behind and straining forward to what lies ahead, I press on toward the goal . . ."*
Here, surely, is a key to Paul's greatness: a wise forgetfulness.
He has learned to use the wastebasket!

He discarded His old path to righteousness; he tossed
away his warped and misplaced zeal as a persecutor of the Christian church..I want to consider what it is that you and I need to
discard; what, for us, deserves the wastebasket.

Well first, let's be clear that there are some things that must never be forgotten: the kindnesses done to us; the people planted along our way who blessed us; the love which from our birth "over and around us lies." None of us can claim to be self-made. We all stand upon the shoulders of giants, and we must never forget it.

But there are some things best forgotten. The hurts and wrongs that we have experienced need to be forgotten. All of us have been injured when we did not deserve to be. In my sophomore year of high school, I was in a biology class taught by one of our football coaches. He was a big man, a transplanted Yankee who loved to project an image of toughness. Our large class was being taught how to use microscopes. The assignment was to get a glass slide of a paramecium, to s Aet it in proper focus, and then to sketch what we saw. It was my first use of a microscope, and as I turned the adjustment wheel to focus on the slide I heard it break. I took it to the teacher to explain my accident. "That'll be thirty-five cents!" he said in an angry voice the whole room could hear. "I don't have thirty-five cents," I said apologetically. "Yeah, that's the trouble with you, Whitaker. You're gonna grow up and have a houseful of kids for the rest of us to take care of!" Everyone heard and I felt the sting of humiliation., which I still feel as I write about it. That teacher injured me in a way that was undeserved. And doubtless you too have been unjustly hurt along the way. Such wrongs must be tossed into the wastebasket. To hold on to a secret file of hurts invites grudges that easily fester into hatred.

Andrew Jackson made a profession of faith late in his life. The minister, who knew of his many feuds, duels, and politically stormy career, asked him pointedly, "General, can you forgive all your enemies?' After a moment of silence, Jackson responded: "My political enemies I can freely forgive; but as for those who abused me when I was serving my country in the field, and those who slandered my wife. . . Doctor, that is a different case." The minister made clear to him that no one who willfully harbored ill feelings against a fellow human being could make a sincere profession of faith. Again, after a thoughtful silence, the aged candidate affirmed that he would try to forgive all his enemies. And so his name was added to the roll of those who always stand in need of a wastebasket.

Hurts have been done to us all, but by us all as well. I once chaperoned a group of our church youth to a gathering called Centrifuge. I attended a group session for adult leaders where we were asked to share personal experiences of being wronged. We were given a chance to hear the ways the others had been wronged. We listened to painful stories of how our new friends had been unjustly hurt. But then our leader added a new twist: "Have you ever committed some hurtful wrong like these just described? With sudden new insight we began to see that we are not only victims of wrong, but are also perpetrators of wrongs. We need not only to forgive but also to be forgiven.

But forgiveness is hard. Corrie Ten Boom survived the Nazi prison at Ravensbruck where her father and sister perished. After the war was over, in 1947, she spoke at large gathering in Munich, proclaiming God's forgiveness for sin to the penitent. After speaking her message of grace she greeted a large number of listeners who wanted to speak their appreciation to her. She saw far down the line a man who had been her guard in the prison. Bitter memories of his cruelty to her and her dead sister filled her mind. He beamed at her when he finally reached her. "A fine message, Fraulein! I have become a Christian, and I know that God has forgiven me for the cruel things I did there, but I would like to hear it from your lips as well. Fraulein, will you forgive me?" He thrust his hand out to her, and an icy coldness gripped her heart. "Jesus, help me!" she prayed silently. Then, in a wooden, mechanical way she shook his hand. Incredibly, she felt a current start in her shoulder, race down her arm to their joined hands. A healing warmth seemed to flood her whole being, and tears filled her eyes. "I forgive you, brother! She cried. "With all my heart." Subsequently, to be sure, she had to renew her forgiveness as painful old memories kept creeping back. But she knew that the only right place for undeserved wrongs was the wastebasket.

The wastebasket is also the place for our failures and missteps. John Mark joined Paul's mission team along with Barnabas, but before they had completed the tour he dropped out and returned home.We are not told why he did this, but Paul refused to take him on a subsequent mission. Barnabas wanted to give him a second chance, but Paul stood firm against it. Their conflict led to a parting of ways. Barnabas took John Mark; Paul took Silas; and two new missions was the result. It would have been easy for Mark to have allowed his poor track record to end his ministry. However, the grace of Barnabas helped him to toss his earlier mission blunder into the wastebasket. By all accounts, he became a true and faithful herald of the gospel. His recovered ministry impressed even Paul, who wrote to Timothy from prison, *"Come soon, and bring Mark with you, for he is useful in my ministry."*

Our failures are never final. I once had a marvelous youth worker, a woman loved and respected by all of our teens. To the surprise of all our church, her own daughter became pregnant some months before high school graduation. Her mother was devastated, and told me she felt she ought to resign her job as a Sunday school teacher of youth. I assured her that her daughter's mistake did not disqualify her as a youth worker or a good mother. She was still held in high esteem in the fellowship of the forgiven. She was able to hear my counsel, and able to throw her perceived failure into the wastebasket.

We need the same trash bin for our painful losses and setbacks, for to love at all is to be vulnerable to loss. C.S. Lewis says it best: "Love anything, and your heart will certainly be wrung and possibly be broken. If you want to make sure of keeping it intact, you must give your heart to no one, not even to an animal." In his novel **Great Expectations**, Dickens tells of Miss Havisham who was jilted at the altar, and could not get over her loss. As an old woman she still wears her faded, yellowed wedding dress; her mantel clock is forever left on the hour of the expected wedding; on her dining table sits the moldy,ruined wedding cake, surrounded by cobwebs and vermin. When the old recluse meets Pip she taps her chest fiercely, and cries, "Broken!" Miss Havisham is a dramatic reminder that our losses, no matter how painful, must go in the wastebasket, lest they control and embitter us. Remember Paul: *"Forgetting that which is behind . . ."* The wastebasket enables life to move on in spiritual health.

Our successes too, need the wastebasket. Why crow about old victories so long that we make ourselves a nuisance? The story is told about a man who'd witnessed the Johnstown flood. It left him with such vivid memories that he spent the rest of his life telling whoever would listen to his tales. People would avoid any mention of the topic. When he died and met St. Peter at the gate, he said, "Let me tell you" — "Stop! said Peter, "Before You say another word, I want you to meet someone. Hey, Noah, come over here a minute!"

L.D. Johnson told the story of the man who found religion after being a notorious carouser. The change was so dramatic that he was always being asked to tell how he got saved. He was so impressed with his victory that he wrote out his conversion experience and stored the paper in the attic for posterity. When a new preacher came to call, the man's wife went to the attic to show him the paper. Shortly she came bounding down the stairs and burst into the parlor aghast. "The mice in the attic have eaten up your experience," she cried. Even our finest victories of the spirit need to be freshened by new experiences.

Guilt often needs the services of the wastebasket. I am not speaking of the positive role guilt plays in leading us to repentance. The son in the far country was entirely right when he decided to say to his father, *"I have sinned against heaven and before you."* That sort of guilt is the friend of grace. I speak of another kind of guilt. Soren Kierkegard's father was convinced that he lived under a curse. As an adolescent he had to shepherd his father's flock , alone on the Danish coast of the North Sea, for days on end. Once, in the bitter cold and consumed by loneliness , he cursed God for his his harsh providence. He believed that anguished curse placed him forever in a state of doom and unforgiveness. How I wish he could have believed that God could forgive a desperately stressed boy for his bitter curse. How I wish he believed there is a wastebasket for neurotic guilt. *"Though your sins be as scarlet, they shall be as white as snow."*

I met a man in a church I served who believed for years that he was unforgivable. He told me that as a boy he heard a preacher say that to speak against "God's anointed" (a preacher), was a sin against the Holy Spirit, and was unforgivable. He remembered that he had once wished a certain preacher would hurry up and quit talking. He became convinced that he had blasphemed and could not be forgiven. Only years later was he able to toss that guilt in the wastebasket.

The Catholic confessional has a valuable insight: never confess the same sin twice. We need not keep confessing the same sin. There is a finality in God's forgiveness. Therefore, the only proper place for the guilt we have confessed is the wastebasket. Thanks be to God who breaks the power of cancelled sin, and sets the prisoner free.

A Call To Kindness

Ephesians 4:31-32

We have all met kindness, and we all want more of it.. Like the man who went to the restaurant. The waitress asked him, "What'll you have?" "Some food and some kind words," he replied. She took his order for a hamburger and when it was ready set it in front of him. "What about the kind words?" he asked. "I wouldn't eat that hamburger if I were you," she said.

When I say the word "kindness," what comes to your mind? An experience when I was five years old comes to mine. My older sister and I were crossing a wide, four-laned boulevard. I was carrying a small bag of peanuts she'had bought, but I dropped them in the middle of that street. Oblivious to the traffic, I stooped and began picking them up. Then I noticed a whole convoy of army trucks were stopped to let me finish picking up. I will never forget the delighted grin of the soldier driving the lead truck. Kindness!

Kindness sticks in the memory like Velcro. It is a central part of the behaving side of our faith. My text is Ephesians 4:32: *"Be kind to one another, tenderhearted, forgiving one another, as God in Christ forgave you."* Notice: our kindness roots in God's own character. He shows us the way. Paul's advice is a perfect echo of Jesus' own teaching: *"But love your enemies, and do good, and lend, expecting nothing in return; and your reward will be great, and you will be sons of the Most High; for he is kind to the ungrateful and the selfish"*. I heard Fred Craddock say that for him, of all the verses in the Bible, this is the verse, the supreme verse. It reveals God's heart of hearts, his essence, his signature, the very Center. For us to approach such gift love is a steep ascent. Get some oxygen! Call in the Sherpas! No wonder Paul describes this kindness toward us in Jesus Christ as *"measureless riches."*

When Paul echoes Jesus' words about kindness, it makes them — in a phrase of Fred Buechner — an air for two voices. No solo here: Jesus says when you love your enemies, do good and lend, you are children of God; Paul says forgive, even as God in Christ has forgiven you. Both issue the call to kindness as an imitation of God himself. We must be copycats! Mimes! We all have felt the pull to imitation as we watch someone we admire. Did you ever watch the grade-school boys at half-time on the football field? They run and block and tackle, imitating their older heroes. I well remember how eagerly I wanted to walk exactly like Wild Bill Elliot after I'd watched him in the picture show. My son John begged to help me push the lawnmower when he was five. Admiration breeds imitation. The clue to the success of mentoring rests in the power of an admirable role model. So, as we gaze upon the divine goodness, kindness is our assignment and our high calling.

What will kindness do? It will purify and grace every relationship. It will not eliminate our hardships, but it will soften the strain of every hard pathway we travel. It will not spare us from every angry encounter, but it will lighten and sometimes redeem them. Kindness will salve the abrasions of life's inevitable frictions.

Paul's summons to behave kindly starts in the heavenlies (Eph. 2:6), but winds up in the T.V. room, the breakfast table, and the workplace. It urges spouses, friends, committee members and kinfolk to be kind. Be kind at school, on the web, on Facebook and behind the wheel. It even asks fellow Christians to be kind at church! I once pastored a church where a painful division had created two major factions who remained stubbornly alienated. I decided I had no option but to address this in a sermon. On the very week before that sermon was preached I came across a serendipitous misprint on a sign in the church basement. Someone had meant to label a storage room there, but had written STORGE ROOM with a magic marker. I almost laughed on the way to my Greek lexicon. Yes, "storge" is one of the Greek words for love or affection. Our church was dying for a storge room, a room bathed in affection! What a happy misprint!

In imitating God's kindness we are called to care as God cares. L.D. Johnson once identified three levels of caring: (1) Inconvenience. The first step of caring is to risk inconvenience. Jesus had an amazing degree of patience with a crowd. Once, after a long day's outdoor teaching session, the disciples, knowing the crowd was hungry, said to their teacher, "Send them away." They didn't want to be bothered. It was an inconvenience. Jesus, however, cared –and you know the story. (2) Involvement. Caring rachets up next to the risk of involvement. Moses was the towering leader and deliverer of God's people. A key moment in his preparation came when he grew up and saw his kinsmen's plight: *"He went out to his people and looked on their burdens."* (Ex. 2:11) Abandoning palace and privilege, he got involved. (3) Identification. The highest level of caring is identification. That means feeling the need of another so keenly that their need becomes my need.

A man was starving in Capri,.
He moved his eyes and looked at me;

I felt his gaze, I heard his moan,
And I knew his hunger as my own.

The call to kindness asks that we care enough to identify, to feel deeply another person's hurt and need. Of course, only God can identify fully. That is the motive force behind the Incarnation. God never loves by remote control, or shouts out helpful swimming instructions to a drowning one: *"Surely he has borne our griefs, and carried our sorrows."* Such is the measure of the divine kindness.

But beware of mushiness; kindness has a stern side too. C.S. Lewis finds my heart with his caveat against kindness as a mere indulgence:

> It is for people whom we care nothing about that we demand happiness on any terms: with our friends, our lovers, our children, we are exacting and would rather see them suffer much than be happy in contemptible and estranging modes. If God is Love, He is, by definition, something more than mere kindness. And it appears, from all the records, that though He has often rebuked us and condemned us, He has never regarded us with contempt. He has paid us the intolerable compliment of loving us, in the deepest, most tragic, most inexorable sense.

Kindness is never a doormat. We err when we think kindness never says no. Kindness can bow up when wronged. It risks the honesty of speaking the unwelcome truth. Coddling wrongdoers, like enabling wrongdoers, is no kindness. To speak the truth in love is a severe but authentic mercy.

Kindness will amplify our Christian witness. A tense and violent world hungers to see real kindness,that unerring pointer to Him, the Unseen Mystery. The Amish folk of Bart Township in Lancaster County, Pennsylvania bear eloquent witness to the way of Jesus. On October 2, 2006 gunman Charles Roberts shot 10 Amish schoolgirls, killing 5 of them before he killed himself. In the face of their shock and grief, that Amish community found ways to live out grace and forgiveness. "We will forgive him," said a grief-stricken family member. An Amish midwife, who had helped at the birth of one of the murdered girls, said, "We're taking food to the family of the gunman." Who can measure the power and pull of such kindness? It shines like light in that tragic darkness.

A final word. Our kindness is not self-generated or self-sustaining. It roots in the everlasting mercy of God himself. We are bathed and immersed in his kindness. The grace we have met in Christ extends help in our own shortage of grace. We draw from his measureless reserves of grace and kindness funds we can never repay. All hail to heaven's bank!

Meeting the Living Christ

Luke 24:13-35

Flora is a gifted Sunday school teacher who has taught adults for many years. When we happened to meet last week she had a question. "Easter is a hard lesson to teach. How do you come up with something new to break into the deadening familiarity of the Resurrection?" I understand her quandary.

Of all the seasonal sermons Easter is my hardest, because everyone knows the story. It is a piece of information, which, for us, can be, for all its flash of arcing voltage in the Gospels, just a dead, blown fuse. It is merely information. Kierkegaard once wrote, "There is no lack of information in a Christian land; something else is lacking." He meant that truth as information alone is dead. It is a cliché, tired, stale, flat. It is possible to "know" the resurrection of Christ without knowing it at all.

A jet airliner prepares to lift off, and a flight attendant stands up front to speak of life or death matters: oxygen masks, emergency exits, flotation devices for a crash over water. But watch the passengers during these life or death instructions. A man reads the Wall Street Journal; a couple laugh at some little story; an old lady with a pillow is catching a nap. The stewardess covers all the dangers, but no one listens. She could be, for a curious moment, an Easter preacher telling the news that is hardly news at all.

Two pictures come to mind when I think of Easter as information. First, I am in pastoral care training at Dorothea Dix Mental Hospital in Raleigh. We students of pastoral ministry are sent to the day room to engage the patients one-on-one in conversation. I meet my troubled patient and after brief introductions I ask her if God seems of any help to her in her situation. Her reply was immediate, as if rehearsed, and in a flat, rapid monotone: "I believe in God the Father, Son and Holy Ghost and in the King James version of the Bible." Period. There seemed no affect, no meaning in her words. Just rattled off like a bored auctioneer.

The second picture is the story of the old Kentucky long rifle that had been passed down in a family for generations as a treasured antique to hang on display above the mantel. The latest owner decided to take the old gun to a gunsmith and have it cleaned up. To everyone's astonishment the gunsmith found that the rifle had for all those years been fully loaded and ready to fire! What seemed to be a harmless showpiece was in fact a loaded,dangerous weapon.

So what is Easter? A safe creedal tenet or a word of explosive power? Our text points the way. It is the story of two disciples of Jesus, who after his death and burial have left Jerusalem and headed for home in Emmaus. It is Sunday afternoon, heading towards sunset, and they are in deep sadness, trudging homeward, talking of the nightmare of Jesus' crucifixion. The time notice of this story is critically important. This is not Good Friday, the day of his death. Nor is it that long, dark Saturday of the tomb. No, this is Sunday afternoon, after Jesus' resurrection! And we learn from their conversation that they had heard the news of resurrection, but were still dispirited and dejected. The women's report was a powerless thing. It was merely a report, a piece of information without lift or life.So long as Easter remains a rumor or a report it makes no vital difference.

Then in this marvelous story the risen Christ, strangely unrecognized, joins them on their journey. *"Their eyes were holden."* To them he was a stranger. Because we know what Cleopas and his unnamed companion do not know, their conversation crackles with dramatic irony. *"We had hoped that he was the one to redeem Israel."* Is there any other sentence in scripture quite so forlorn? The words are freighted with the grief of broken dreams. *"We had hoped."* When resurrection is only a rumor, broken dreams stay broken. So they trudge toward home, prepared to live in their own strength, bracing themselves to endure trouble and tragedy as best they could.

This old road is often our road too. Modern disciples sometimes trudge this dusty way, choked with grief, late in the day. Emmaus is seven miles from Jerusalem, but its not so much a place as it is a mood. Emmaus is wherever life has fallen in; where dreams have died, and hope is gone.

Like family life, so rife with scary rapids. How easily can breaches develop between parents and a son or daughter. I well remember a large Family Life Conference in Nashville years ago. The Clinebells—Howard and Charlotte—were leading us with skill and wisdom through the briar patches of family dysfunction. But in an unscheduled free time gathering they opened their hearts to a few of us."Our own daughter is nineteen. Things are bad just now between us. We're trying, but we're just not getting through." It happens to the experts; it happens to us all.

Perhaps someone trudges today with a marriage tumbling in. James Fowler, professor of theology and human development at Emory University, told of a meeting in New York with a well-known novelist. He asked the writer to share his views of the essence of human beings. The novelist, who had his own questions and agenda with Fowler, impatiently tossed off his reading of life: "Everything runs down. Your body runs down, your creativity runs down, your marriage runs down." Yes.

Maybe you slog on to Emmaus, bearing broken hopes of some treasured goal. A certain school; a certain job; a certain person. We joke about the loves of youth that crash and burn, but do you recall how it felt to love someone who did not love you back?

It could be that your path is where one of the "natural shocks that flesh is heir to" has rudely interrupted everything. Life-threatening news about your health; the death of one who cannot be replaced. Emily Dickinson once wrote, "My life closed twice before its close,"and we sense what she must have meant.

I wonder about those who drop out of church entirely. They remember the days when God's service was joyous and bracing, but they have now checked out as thoroughly as P.T.A. parents whose last child is finally out of school.

On all such roads we need to meet the living Christ. Heavy hearts long for a presence. Oscar Wilde cried out once when his heart was "as some famine-murdered land:"

> *Come down O Christ and help me! Reach thy hand,*
> *For I am drowning in a stormier sea*
> *Than Simon on thy lake of Galilee.*

The truth of our scripture text is that the living Christ does come to us. Sometimes in a flash of worship; sometimes in un-expected rendezvous on our daily path. He finds our roads and falls in step.

I once preached a revival in New Roads, Louisiana. I have never forgotten that fitting name, for the risen Christ indeed makes all roads new. He leads us from our old roads to his new roads. Some are on wrong roads today: dead end roads; rocky roads; ill-chosen roads. You may hope he will bless your deadly trails, but he will not. He offers only roads that lead to life.

The two disciples of Emmaus invited the incognito Christ to be their guest when they reached home. When they ate supper together Christ broke bread, blessed it, and gave it to them. Immediately their eyes were opened in recognition, and then he vanished. They were convinced of resurrection not by earlier information but by his vital presence: *"Did not our hearts burn within us while he talked with us on the road, while he opened for us the scriptures?"*

Robert McAfee Brown tells a powerful story of resurrection in the Mid-Pacific. He was chaplain on a ship bringing 1,500 marines back from Japan to the U.S. For discharge after World War II. To his amazement a small group of them asked him to lead a Bible study class each morning.

Toward the end of the trip the group read the eleventh chapter of John, which describes the raising of Lazarus from the dead. The chaplain suggested that the incident dramatized what Jesus said on that occasion: *"I am the resurrection and the life: he that believeth in me, though he were dead, yet shall he live: and whosoever liveth and believeth in me shall never die."* More important even than the reanimation of a corpse in A.D.30 was the question of whether or not that statement of Jesus was true in (what was then) A.D. 1946. He told them the story of Raskolnikov, a man in Dostoevsky's **Crime and Punishment** who had killed his very self in the act of murdering another, but had in truth been brought back to life as these words of Jesus were read to him.There was little discussion. A couple of questions were raised, but on the whole there was nothing to indicate to the chaplain that he had made his point particularly well.

When the discussion was over, a Marine corporal followed the chaplain back to his cabin. After a few false starts he got down to the point. "Chaplain," he said, "I felt as though everything we read this morning was pointed right at me. I've been living in hell for the last six months, and for the first time I feel as though I'd gotten free." As he talked, the story came out. He had just finished high school when he was called into the service. He had spent a long time in the occupation forces in Japan. He had gotten bored. Finally he had gone off one night with some friends and gotten into trouble. Serious trouble. Fortunately (so he thought) no one else knew about it.

But he knew about it. And he was sure God knew about it. He felt guilty, terribly guilty. And each day as the ship got nearer to San Francisco, his feeling increased that he had ruined his life and that he would never be able to face his family back home. But somehow that wasn't the end, after all. He kept repeating one idea over and over again: "Up until today, Chaplain, I've been a dead man. I have felt utterly condemned by myself, by my family (if they knew), and by God. I've been dead, but now, after reading about Jesus and Lazarus, I know that I am alive again. The forgiveness of God can reach even to me. The resurrection Jesus was talking about is real, after all, right now."

When the corporal left the cabin, it was clear that he still had a lot of problems to iron out, and that things wouldn't automatically be easy in this "new life," but as the chaplain watched him go, he knew that on that day, on that ship, in the middle of the Pacific Ocean, the miracle of resurrection had taken place. It was quite evident that Jesus' words were true: *"He that believeth in me, though he were dead, yet shall he live."*

This risen Christ who gives the miracle of new life on our pathway is able also to give eternal life in the face of our last enemy death. I recently sat with a dying friend. It was cancer and he had fought it bravely. They had given him strong chemotherapy until it shut his kidneys down. Then they told him they had done all they could, and would try to keep him comfortable at home. He had always been a positive person, looking on the promising side of any situation. Now, reduced to a ghastly thinness except for a large, swollen belly, he was beginning to accept his approaching death. "I just don't know how long I've got. It could be a week; could be a month; could be—I don't know-- maybe even six months." His present weakness seemed strange, for he had always been in robust health.. He walked around in shirtsleeves in the cold North Georgia winters. "It's hard to accept. I'd never been sick a day in my life. Then a month before I retired, they found this. We had all these plans to travel. I've been working since I was a boy."

We sat with periods of silence. Grief and the acceptance of a hard reality was the task before us. We talked of the hope in Christ that shines in the shadow of death. We prayed, commending his care to a loving Father, asking for grace and courage, and help in the time of need. He thanked me for coming with glistening eyes. We shook hands and I walked out into the night.

It was there that it hit me, for the sudden beauty of the night flashed before me. The glittering lights on White Oak Mountain, stretching as far down Taylor's Ridge as the eye could see, was stunning. The town lay like a fairyland of lights down in the valley. Overhead the silent stars burned with silver eyes.

But I refused to be seduced by the loveliness of the night. For if all of earth's beauty is destined at last to slip over the abyss into death, if the slow, sure doom, pitiless and dark, marks time over all our hopes, if the last road finally just heads toward Emmaus and the gathering night, then we have no lasting hope. But I choose to believe that we can meet the living Christ on our own roads of loss and anguish. And I believe he meets us on the last road of all. This living Christ gives to us the promise of life through him. *"Because I live you shall live also."* (John 14:19) Not a rumor, not a report, but a living vital, presence that transforms life and death. That is the living Christ!

Our Bethels and Their Climax

John 1:51

I know a place where a white frame church once sat. It was on the north side of Sarasota, on the Old Bradenton Road, dotted with palmettos, sandspurs, and working-class houses. Bay Haven Baptist Church is its name, and it is a holy place in my memories. There, in that wooden-frame church I was baptized; there I sat in Sunday school class; there at age sixteen I preached my first sermon. That church was my Bethel, "house of God." Whenever I return to it, for me, it is back to Bethel . . .

Do you know how we got that name? It goes back to Jacob, the ambitious twin and mama's boy, who, by her thorough coaching, tricked his twin Esau out of his rightful inheritance. It was a shabby masquerade that took advantage of his doddery father's failing eyesight. He dressed up like Esau, deceived his old father, and secured the first-born's blessing. Of course Esau found out and swore to undo Jacob's triumph by killing him. Jacob's only safety was to flee, so he fled, alone with his oppressive inner baggage: guilt, fear and self-loathing. When night fell he found a stone for a pillow and drifted into a fitful sleep. Then came an astonishing dream: a ladder stretched from earth to heaven, with the angels of God ascending and descending in unceasing traffic. Then a voice: *"I am the God of your fathers; the land you lie on will be yours; your offspring will be like the numberless dust, and will bless the whole earth's peoples. I am with you and I will keep you; I'll bring you back to this place and will never leave you."* (Genesis 28:13-15)

Jacob awakened with a start! *"Surely the Lord is in this place and I didn't know it."* With a sense of shuddering awe he cried, *"This is none other than the house of God* ("Beth-el") *and this is the gate of heaven."* So there—all unexpected and undeserved—a ladder was lowered, and the rich mercies of God gladdened the lonely wilderness.

This marvelous story persuades me that we can meet God anywhere. No wonder John took this story of heaven's ladder lowered to earth as his frontispiece for Jesus' ministry in his book of signs. At the Gospel's beginning, as Jesus gathers his disciples, he promises Nathanael "You will see heaven opened, and the angels of God ascending and descending upon the Son of Man." In his saving work new Bethels would appear around them everywhere, and Jesus himself would be the ladder. John is on fire to tell the story of that ministry. His Gospel's Book of Signs brims with encounters of grace: A woman—at Jacob's well, of all places—hears of new and living water. "He slakes my thirst!, she cries joyously to the whole town. Bethel's ladder had dropped anew. In Jerusalem a man born blind declares to the yet-more-blind establishment, "He lets me see!" In Bethany where Lazarus lay a stiff, decaying corpse, again a ladder drops: When Jesus calls him to life from out of the tomb, they can only conclude "He is the resurrection and the life!"

Everywhere he brought new Bethels of marvel and surprise. In Christ, heaven's plenty met earth's scarcity. Down all the centuries those Bethels never ceased. Our Christian story teems with vital, saving encounters. In bright, incandescent moments the living Christ has kept becoming a ladder of grace: to Saul en route to Damascus; to Augustine in his garden of anguish; to Wesley at a Bible study on Aldersgate Street; to C.S.Lewis on a drive to Whipsnade; to Eldridge Cleaver on his Mediterranean balcony of moonlit despair.

Bethels everywhere. But yours?...Where? Our Bethels, like politics, are always local. When the Lord appeared to Abraham by the oaks of Mamre, I believe it was so local and concrete that he could feel the acorns beneath his sandals. When God called Amos he was in Tekoa dressing the sycamore trees. His fingertips felt the fruit of that place even as the ladder dropped from the eternal habitations. Francis Thompson felt the immediate presence in his own London anguish:

> *But, when so sad thou canst not sadder,*
> *Cry;—and upon thy so sore loss*
> *Shall shine the traffic of Jacob's ladder*
> *Pitched betwixt Heaven and Charing Cross.*
> *The Bethel-Christ can come to us wherever we may*
> *Cry-- clinging Heaven by the hems;*
> *And lo, Christ walking on the water,*
> *Not of Gennesareth, but Thames!*
> Francis Thompson, No Strange Land

God in Christ met me both in the sandy palmetto-land of my Gulf-coast boyhood, and in the red Georgia clay of my manhood as well. Christ walks the waters of Longboat Key or the Chattahoochee. He comes to our locales.

> *You see, I know a secret place in that white frame church where the Maker of me "almost unmade, what with dread" his doing.*
> G.M.Hopkins, The Wreck of the Deutschland

In an overwhelming experience of call to ministry, when I was eleven years old, came that ladder, holy, radiant, unearthly. I know another place: Seminary chapel, Wake Forest, North Carolina, where in 1963, decked out in cap and gown, I sang with the others Dr. McDowell's Seminary Hymn:

> *Ordained of God his prophets rise,*
> *They seek not gain nor earthly prize;*
> *They heed the challenge of Christ's call,*
> *They ask to give and spend their all.*

With the organ soaring its holy ranges my soul was all but out of me,and the ladder descended. I celebrate such holy glimpses, fleeting as they are. They serve as counter-poise to the desolations of His absence, the crushing silences.

Our brief Bethels whet the appetite. "More," we cry, with Moses, Job or Jeremiah to the elusive Presence. Moses is portrayed in Exodus as conversing face to face with God. But still there remained an aching absence. Why else would he plead, *"Show me your glory"*? And why else would the Lord allow him to see only the briefest glimpse of his backside? *"You cannot see my face; for man shall not see me and live."* (Ex.33:20)

The writer to the Hebrews saw the hunger for "more"in Abram's wanderlust. Leaving Haran behind, he went to Canaan as he was led, but that piece of ground was not his real goal. He was searching for *"a city with foundations whose builder and maker was God."* He sought that elusive Presence which is both our hunger and our salvation. Emilie Griffin says it so tellingly:

> . . . there is a desire within us for something greater than ourselves, a hunger which we ourselves can never satisfy. To see this for the first time is to feel a sudden isolation, a sudden helplessness. . is to know all at once that we

can never provide for ourselves, under our own power,
our own fulfillment. We see that we are not enough for
ourselves, by ourselves; and that others—friends, wives,
husbands, lovers—cannot satisfy us in that deepest part
of ourselves where this heartfelt longing dwells.

(Turning, p. 46)

I have come to believe that our fleeting Bethels that long
for more are at bottom a longing for home. Home in the deepest
sense of where we truly belong. In my father's old age he would
just strike out from home, walking down the long gravel road
that ran by our house. When asked where he was going he would
answer, "Home." I think he was looking for that Georgia farm-
place where he grew up.But was it merely dementia? Of course
it was dementia, but I choose to think it may have sprung from a
deeper, God-planted nostalgia as well. G.K.Chesterton wrote of
the place:

To an open house in the evening
Home shall men come,
To an older place than Eden
And a taller town than Rome;

The Bible saves for its climax the final vision of John
where the Seer describes a whole new heaven and a new earth.
There, at the end of all our roads, the glad, unbroken presence of
God will replace all brief and fleeting Bethels of our past. There
the climax of our deepest yearning, a true, true Bethel awaits:

And I heard a loud voice from the throne saying,
Behold the dwelling of God is with men.
He will dwell with them, and they shall be his people,
and God himself will be with them; he will wipe away
every tear from their eyes, and death shall be no more.

(Revelation 21:3-4)

The Way of Christ

Made in the USA
Middletown, DE
05 March 2020